Elizabeth:
the feisty feminist

Mary Holmes

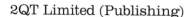

2QT Limited (Publishing)

First Edition published 2022 by
2QT Limited (Publishing)
Settle, N. Yorkshire

Cover image: Supplied by Mary Evans Picture Library

Printed by IngramSpark

A CIP catalogue record for this book is available
from the British Library

ISBN 978-1-914083-58-7

Contents

The author uses both footnotes and endnotes in the chapter text. The footnotes are highlighted with an asterisk, and the reference or comment is placed at the bottom of the page. The endnotes are identified with a number and the reference or comment is found on pages 165 to 171.

Acknowledgements

Each year, Fulneck Settlement holds an Open Heritage Day. In 2018 Myra Dickinson asked me to prepare a window display about the suffragettes, and that was when I discovered Elizabeth Wolstenholme Elmy.

With encouragement and interest from Fulneck folk, I learned more about her. Dr Maureen Wright and the Elizabeth Group were helpful as I explored Elizabeth's life in more depth. A visit to Ian at the Congleton Museum was very informative and led to my introduction to Peter and Mandy, who are proud to live in the house on Buxton Road that was once home to the adult Elizabeth and her family. Peter and Mandy, plus their dogs, were kind enough to show me around the house. It all felt so real, and it was a wonderful experience.

As I committed myself to writing a book, I realised I needed an editor. After a long search, I came across 2QT: over the months, Karen and Catherine have offered guidance and shared their wealth of knowledge.

Throughout all this, I have needed encouragement, support, feeding, and sometimes driving around. John, my wonderful husband, has always been there to offer whatever was needed. Without him I can safely say that the idea would not have come to fruition.

Thanks to you all – to my friends and to many others who have played their part in contributing to this book.

◆ ◆ ◆

Elizabeth dedicated her life to women's rights, so it only feels right that all profits should go to charities supporting women's rights. For details, please see the end of the book.

Glossary

ACLL	Anti-Corn Law League
CALIPIW	Campaign for Amending the Law in Points wherein it is Injurious to Women (also see PRA)
CDAs	Contagious Diseases Acts
EWJ	*English Woman's Journal*
LNA	Ladies National Association for the repeal of the CDAs
MWPA	Married Women's Property Act
NAPSS	National Association for the Promotion of Social Science
NUWSS	National Union of Women's Suffrage Society
PRA	Personal Rights Association (the name taken on by CALIPIW after a few years)
SPEW	Society for the Promotion of Employment for Women (renamed many years later as Futures for Women)
WEU	Women's Emancipation Union
WFL	Women's Franchise League
WSPU	Women's Social and Political Union

Introduction

The nineteenth century became the crucible for change in women's rights. Born in 1833, Elizabeth Wolstenholme Clarke Elmy was a significant pioneer in this movement. She dedicated her life to changing many aspects of how women could live, then and now. Her overarching passion was for a fair and just society where women shared equally in all aspects of life.

> *The emancipation of women is a ... question [which] strikes down to the roots of social, political and religious life ... to secure true freedom women of all classes need to unite themselves in one great federation [to] fight male tyranny.*[1]

Fighting male tyranny in its many forms was fundamental to the women's movement in which Elizabeth was a key player. Throughout the nineteenth century, these women and their male supporters were a vital part of the sweeping changes that were transforming Victorian and Edwardian society. The movement sought to challenge the confinement and injustices faced by women and Elizabeth, along with many others, fought valiantly to bring about a change in the perception and reality of women's lives. By the time of her death, Elizabeth had significantly influenced many changes in the law, from which we still benefit, and had laid down markers for work that is continuing to this day.

My aim is to set her achievements within the context of a changing world and to celebrate how the role of women was emerging. Such achievements demanded a lifetime of effort supported by an understanding of how to engage and involve others. Elizabeth became renowned for her use of the word, both spoken and printed. Throughout her life she wrote many articles and pamphlets, and thousands of letters. As she recognised – and capitalised on – the power of the pen, I have drawn upon various publications from the period.

Newspapers and periodicals were expanding as education became more widespread. Novels exposed middle- and upper-class women to the lives of women who had to work in the mills, the fields – and possibly as their own servants – in order to survive. Periodicals became more popular and addressed a range of topics, including the cause of women's rights.

Following the first French Revolution, people were discussing radical new ideas and fighting for power, talking about their rights and demanding change. Science was driving forward an understanding of the world and opening up new ways of working and of communicating; in turn, this led to a questioning of religion. It was into this turbulent, changing world that Elizabeth was born.

Within this turbulent world, even women wanting to improve their lives were divided. Some felt getting the vote was the first step; others wanted to see many social and political changes for women – education, financial independence, equality in marriage and much more.

Elizabeth was most definitely of the latter opinion but,

despite this, she agreed that emancipation was vital. She helped found the fight and was fully signed up to the suffragist cause; later she accepted the more proactive suffragette stance that involved direct militant action.

Where to start with this book? I have begun with a broadbrush view of the dramatically changing world into which Elizabeth was born, then focussed on her young life to highlight aspects that may have informed how she grew up to become a 'feisty feminist'.

'Remarkable life story of town's feisty feminist' was the title of an article in the local Congleton* newspaper in 2006. The opening sentences stated that:

Of all those who have campaigned for equality between the sexes, none whose lives have been more influential have remained in the shadows as much as Elizabeth Wolstenholme Elmy.[2]

Feisty can be a contentious word, proving that language changes as the world moves on. Is it acceptable to describe Elizabeth as feisty? Stay with the word, and we can revisit its use at the end of the book.

I have drawn on contemporary written accounts from many sources to illustrate Elizabeth's many achievements. Each of her campaigns shows her determination to speak out against injustice. Taken as a whole, her lifetime's work shows a breadth of concerns and an appreciation of how dire the situation was for many women because of several interrelated factors. She firmly believed that there was no single issue that could be addressed to change the world.

Next, I look at Elizabeth's life in Congleton, including the active and practical support she received from her

---

* Elizabeth lived much of her adult life in Congleton.

lifelong partner, Ben Elmy. Finally, I examine her legacy to the world of women's rights and consider how her work continues today.

Throughout the book, I introduce many people who worked alongside Elizabeth because, although the focus is on her achievements, no single person can bring about such a radical shift.

In her book *The Petticoat Rebellion*, Ramelson offers a succinct summary of Elizabeth's life and work.

Elizabeth Wolstenholme Elmy's long and arduous life's work was devoted to establishing that women should enjoy both the same rights and duties as men and that these should be clearly established as to leave no dubiety that every woman was in control of her person, property, her actions, her earnings and her children.[3]

Chapter 1: Setting the scene

History has too frequently marginalised influential women from all walks of life. Elizabeth Wolstenholme Elmy felt marginalised from an early stage in her life, yet she challenged laws and had a significant impact on all our lives.

Elizabeth was born in a northern city at a time when the Industrial Revolution was in full flow. She was surrounded by poverty and grew up in a society where divisions between workers and mill owners were firing up radicalism. Her mother died in childbirth. Her brother received a good higher education, but that was denied to his intelligent, inquisitive sister because she was a girl. Newspapers and books were starting tentatively to explore women's rights.

Result? We have one feisty feminist.

Meet a feisty feminist

Elizabeth was a Manchester girl who studied at Fulneck School, near Leeds. After two years there, she worked as a governess then moved back to Manchester and on to Congleton, where she lived for most of her life. She became one of the most influential Victorian feminists.

Can we call her a feisty feminist? There are many

definitions of a feminist; I suspect that Elizabeth would have agreed with Margaret Atwood's view that women are 'complete, equal and flawed'.

Elizabeth fought for equality, and certainly some of her contemporaries considered her flawed because of her strong opinions. She was often challenged by those who disagreed with her views on marriage, religion and many other topics. At times she was argumentative. However, she was true to her beliefs and was supported by her lifelong partner, Ben Elmy, who was also a strong advocate for equality.

If she were alive today, it is likely that Elizabeth would concur with the Fawcett Society website, which states that it aims for:

> A society in which women and girls in all their diversity are equal and truly free to fulfil their potential creating a stronger, happier, better future for us all.[1]

The society was established in 1866 by Millicent Garrett Fawcett, and their aim today echoes words Elizabeth wrote in later life in her publication, *Women and the Law**. This was a major influence in defining citizenship so that it encompassed *all* women, regardless of class, race, ethnicity or religion. However, although Fawcett and Elizabeth were both passionate about women getting the vote, there were other areas where they disagreed strongly, particularly in discussions about sexuality.

For fifty-two years Elizabeth tirelessly guided the cause of women's rights, and her campaigns for social, legal

---

* *Women and the Law: a series of four letters.* Elizabeth Wolstenholme Elmy. Published by the Women's Emancipation Union, 1896.

and political equality shaped many of the rights and laws women take for granted today. Current laws in this country allow women to live independently and follow educational, personal and career goals, freedoms that were denied to Victorian women.

She had a significant impact on what women can do:

› vote
› stand for public office
› keep the money they earn
› own property in their own name
› have an education and gain qualifications
› work in a profession
› choose how they live (be single, married or live with a partner)
› have responsibility for their own children
› have legal protection against domestic violence.

Elizabeth had the courage to wade into the thorny topic of physical violence against women and to speak openly about marital rape, a horror that many women experienced. This subject was never discussed, especially by women and *never* in public. At the time, it was accepted that women belonged to their fathers until they were 'given' to their husbands in marriage, and that their husbands could beat them if they judged it appropriate. It was regarded as justifiable for a man to control his wife. Elizabeth's work was pivotal in challenging domestic violence.

A timeline of her work, shown in Appendix 1, offers some impression of her tireless efforts. I feel exhausted just reading it, particularly considering that she taught full time from 1854 until 1871 and had more connections through her written correspondence than many of us manage with social media.

Radical Manchester

Elizabeth was born in Manchester in 1833, a city that had grown rapidly since the beginning of the Industrial Revolution as mills and mines demanded more workers. Political unrest was common, and this was fired up in the 1830s by various laws that stoked anger among the working classes.

Manchester was physically and socially divided between the wealthy mill owners who lived in beautiful homes and their workers who existed in squalid, overcrowded conditions. The masters and men faced each other with hostility as tension and resentment filled the workplaces. While the mill owners were interested in profits and protecting their privileged lifestyles, the workers cared about conditions and pay. Conflict was bubbling and Manchester was becoming the home of economic radicalism.

The French Revolution had stimulated interest in, and discussion about, liberty and freedom. Then, after the Napoleonic wars, there was a major economic slump that led to significant unemployment, together with harvest failures and the introduction of the Corn Laws that kept the price of bread high. Ten years before Elizabeth was born, these and other grievances led to an event in Manchester that was a game changer: what started as a peaceful rally turned into the Peterloo Massacre on 16 August 1819.

A large crowd had gathered to make clear their demands. Having poured in from Bolton, Bury, Rochdale and other nearby towns, they were in a cheerful mood. As their banners flew calling for liberty, votes and lower taxes, they were expecting a day of laughter and fun.

Henry Hunt, a charismatic orator, addressed the rally before the violence broke out.

In 2012, *The Guardian* called this rally 'the bloody clash that changed Britain'. In his article, Bates set out the reasons behind it:

> On the face of it, a Monday morning in August was a strange time to hold a political rally. Most factory workers would be at their machines – the deafening, ceaseless clacking cotton spinning machinery that ran in the mills day and night. An industry was taking off: there were 2,400 power looms locally in 1813; 14,000 by 1820 and 115,000 within 15 years. But the handloom weavers, who worked from home and traditionally took Mondays off after working all weekend, were available. They were still in the majority in the Lancashire cotton trade: 40,000 in Manchester alone, compared to 20,000 spinning-machine operatives in the factories – but they feared for their jobs, skills, lifestyles and standards of living. Wages had halved since the end of the Napoleonic war: 12 shillings a week for 16-hour days, if you could get the work: a decade earlier, it had been 21 shillings a week.[2]

The peaceful protest turned bloody when a magistrate ordered troops to break up the crowd. Nobody could have envisaged their vicious and violent response. The Manchester Yeomanry attacked the crowd of sixty thousand, leaving fifteen dead and more than one hundred injured.

The recently formed society calling for the female vote, the forerunner of the suffragist movement in which Elizabeth would lead the way, had encouraged women who were attending to dress in white as a symbol of purity because too often they were ridiculed in the press as sluts and whores. Being in white, they were easily spotted by the troops and suffered particularly badly; the view of the troops was that if women wanted to be equal to men, they must share in the treatment being meted out to men. This was a foretaste of the treatment handed out to suffragettes in later years.

Henry Hunt, a charismatic orator, addressed the rally before the violence broke out. Although he was immediately imprisoned following the rally, he wrote to a local newspaper stating that he had never seen people more disposed to be peaceful. By the time Henry Hunt's letter appeared in print on the Saturday after the rally, he was in New Bailey Prison, Manchester, on charges of high treason. He wrote that those who had attacked the people would find that:

The blood of the poor murdered people sits heavy on their heads, and will haunt the guilty souls as long as they live.[3]

Hunt remained dedicated to the cause, and by 1830 was the MP for Preston. You will meet him again soon – on his horse.

Time did not heal the hurt and anger caused by the Peterloo Massacre, and it was still being talked about in the 1830s when Elizabeth was growing up. Conditions deteriorated during the same decade, and by 1837 about 50,000 workers in the city were unemployed. The wages of handloom weavers fell significantly; by 1830, they were earning about ten shillings a week less than they had in 1815. Young Elizabeth witnessed this hardship and the unrest it caused; times were indeed hard, and many laws were particularly unpopular.

The Chartist Movement developed in Manchester to lobby for the vote so that men could influence wages, factory conditions, working and living standards. In 1780, only 3% of the population of the country could vote, and large cities such as Manchester had no MP. Working men were demanding change and their resentment focussed on two laws: the 1832 Reform Act, which was seen as only giving more votes to middle-class men, and the 1834 Poor Law, which added to the woes of those already in dire need.

The 1832 Reform Act vested the right to vote (and therefore the right to citizenship) in 'male persons', thus stating clearly that it excluded females. Power and political control were legally placed within the hands of men – and radical Victorian women challenged this exclusion from the public arena.

The 1834 Poor Law withdrew financial relief and drove people into workhouses, where conditions were atrocious. Having worked in the Manchester mills, Friedrich Engels wrote *The Condition of the Working Class in England* when Elizabeth was a young girl.

Engels visited the New Bridge Street Workhouse and its environs. Elizabeth grew up very close to it and would have known people who ended up there. Engels said it was the 'Poor Law Bastille of Manchester' and described how the building, with its high walls and parapets, looked down threateningly from a hilltop upon the workers' quarter below.

Engels describes the torrid conditions in which people

struggled to live, the crowded dwellings where:

sick and well sleep in the same room, in the same bed, the only wonder is that a contagious disease, like the fever, does not spread further.[4]

As they faced unemployment and wage cuts, men and women struggled to keep out of the workhouse. This was happening at a time when mill owners were seeking women and children to work for them because they could pay them less.

Women and children soon became the majority workforce in the Lancashire cotton mills and at the pit bottoms in the coal mines. In 1842, a report into working conditions in the mines included stories from fathers of how they had to lift sacks onto the backs of their wives and children: these sacks were so heavy the men ruptured themselves. Between the Poor Law and the working conditions, women and children were being worked to the point of physical and mental exhaustion. It is little wonder that death rates were so high.

The memory of the injustices that led to, and occurred at, Peterloo was kept strong by the ongoing suffering and divisions within the city. It stirred people up to challenge unjust laws, of which the unpopular Corn Laws were top of their list. The fight against them, and the ultimate success in repealing them, had a strong influence on Elizabeth's childhood.

The *Manchester Times*, January 1831 states:

If the world's history were looked through, there would not – with the single exception of negro* slavery – be

---

*   This word is no longer in use but is included here as quoting from the original text.

found so glaring and huge an instance of the abuse of
power, and the general misery consequent on giving
one selfish class the right of legislation for the rest, as is
presented by the commercial policy of this most ill-used
country.[5]

This article included a report on a great procession in Bolton against the Corn Laws. Like Peterloo, there was music and flag waving. Mr Henry Hunt, now the celebrated local MP, rode through town on a horse. During a speech at a dinner later that day, he was described in glowing terms as *'the same man when bloody sabre waved over his head at Peterloo...'*

History had not been forgotten and new heroes were being created. Some newspapers were there to rally support for causes dear to their readers' hearts.

Elizabeth was born into this politically radical environment. Her neighbours went to these rallies, talked about these matters in the crowded yards, and worshipped at services led by her father. As she learned to read, she gained a broader understanding of the factors that made life hard, especially for women, and started to develop her ability to see connections between them.

The power of the pen and the press

Elizabeth, along with many nineteenth-century feminists, fully appreciated the power of the pen and the press. Without the option of email and social media, they took to ink and print to keep in touch, to engage in discussion and to stimulate debate. There was a wealth of public and private letters shared by these women, used to raise a range of topics and explore views.

During the nineteenth century, daily and weekly news-papers were increasing their distribution and growing the influence they had upon public opinion. By 1892, there were seventy-four daily morning papers and eighty-five evening papers in the UK. This shows the great thirst for inform-ation about politics, social change and international affairs.

The press was dominated by men and so it was largely silent, or scathing, on the topic of women's rights. By the 1850s, just as young Elizabeth was entering the world of work, feminists were beginning to find a voice by tapping into the thriving market for periodicals. As her campaigning grew over the years, we will see how she made use of these to get her voice heard through the power of her pen; she wrote powerfully and encouraged action to achieve her aims. From these female writers came the voice of the diverse women's movement. They aimed to stimulate discussion, encourage debate and point towards concrete political action.

In 1858, the first publication of the *English Women's Journal* (EWJ) appeared and went on to be judged as having a fundamental role in bringing the feminist movement into existence in the 1860s. It picked up regularly on the theme of women's employment, emphasising the dignity that could come with employment and the need for broader opportunities for women to enter work.

Over the next few years, other periodicals appeared. Some took a broad view of feminism while others focused upon a single topic. For example, *Shield* was purely for writing related to the campaign for the removal of the Contagious Diseases Acts, and the *Women's Suffrage*

Journal fought only for the vote.

These periodicals were not just about radical feminism. The *Kettledrum* came out in 1869 with the playful explanation that *'tea-table talk and tea-table interests will be here discussed and nothing more.'* [6] However, behind the light-hearted approach were some serious discussions. They raised the matter that the English custom of drinking tea was founded on the practice of providing the growers with opium in exchange for their crop rather than payment in money. Tea was often drunk with sugar; again, they did not shy away from highlighting that sugar would most likely have been grown on plantations worked by slaves.

Despite the growing voice of feminists, it was not until the late 1860s that other journals took such views seriously. Perhaps not surprisingly, the shift was led by a man, John Stuart Mill.

Women were divided about engaging with MPs and with men in general: some did not wish to connect with men while others believed human equality meant working as equals with them. Elizabeth was in the latter camp; much of her work illustrates how she successfully engaged with, and influenced, men across all classes. Nonetheless, male domination continued for years to come in the press, society and politics.

You can't teach a cat to crochet

In her dystopian novel *The Testaments*, Margaret Atwood offers an explanation to a young girl about masculine power.

...going into my father's study was forbidden.

What my father was doing in there was said to be very

important – the important things men did, too important for females to meddle with because they had smaller brains that were incapable of thinking large thoughts, according to Aunt Vilada, who taught us Religion. It would be like trying to teach a cat to crochet, said Aunt Estee, who taught Crafts, and that would make us laugh, because how ridiculous! Cats didn't even have fingers.[7]

Had Elizabeth read this, it would have resonated with her experiences. In the nineteenth century, the prevailing view was the patriarchal model of power. Mary Beard highlights that a radical separation – real, cultural and imaginary – between women and power goes far back into Western history. During Elizabeth's lifetime, women gradually started to challenge their exclusion from political, social and economic power.

When she was young, the predominant view was that women were naive, fragile and emotionally weak so they needed guidance and support from the males in their lives. The lives of men and women were also divided along class lines. Middle-class men and women operated in different spheres, with women knowing only the restrictions of the home and the responsibilities of keeping a man happy. In contrast, working-class were women exposed to the hardships of manual labour in the fields, the mills and the mines.

For all women, the marital bed was regarded as a place of duty not of pleasure. In 1857 a renowned physician, Acton, wrote that females generally do not feel sexual excitement and do not desire sexual gratification for themselves.

The best mothers, wives and managers of households, know little or nothing of sexual indulgences. Love of home, children, and domestic duties are the only passions they feel.[8]

Religion was a fundamental part of life at the time, yet questions were raised about the Anglican Church's practice of confession. Husbands were the head of the house and some saw it as a threat that their wives would speak in private to a priest. Heavens – they might tell them things that they did not tell their husband!

By 1877, a book entitled *The Priest and Absolution* had addressed this matter. In response *The Times* published several articles, and *Punch* had fun with a cartoon titled *'A Wolf in sheep's clothing'*. By this time Elizabeth had renounced religion, but she was probably still enraged that woman who wished to follow their religion might have their practices and freedom curtailed.

By the 1870s, women such as Elizabeth had raised the issue of women's rights to a point where it was becoming more mainstream. Some women – and men – were starting to move from the concept of male supremacy to the more modern notion of gender equality.

John Stuart Mill, a politician and highly influential British philosopher, wrote a polemic *The Subjection of Women* in 1867, in which he states:

How early the youth thinks himself superior to his mother, owing her forbearance perhaps but no real respect; and how sublime and sultan-like a sense of superiority he feels, above all, over the woman whom he honours by admitting her to a partnership of his life. Is it imagined that all this does not pervert the whole manner of existence of the man, both as an individual and as a social being?[9]

Frances Power Cobbe, one of the few females of this period to gain employment in mainstream journalism, published more than twenty books and wrote extensively on a range of topics. In *The Duties of Women*, first published in 1881, she entered the debate about women and their role, clearly expressing the view that women can retain virtues while taking on new rights.

> *If women were to become less dutiful by being enfranchised, - less conscientious, less unselfish, less temperate, less chaste, - then I should say: 'For heaven's sake, let us stay where we are. Nothing we can ever gain would be worth such a loss.' But I have yet to learn that freedom, which is the spring of all nobler virtues in man, will be less the ground of loftier and purer virtues in women.*[10]

Debates raged about what gaining new rights would mean for men, women and society in general, debates with which Elizabeth was keen to engage. She also wanted to see clear action as she guided to fruition the emerging rights that were being gained, but this was still set within the context of some firmly entrenched views.

Many people still held traditional views about women's roles being to bear children and tend to the needs of their husbands. They regarded women as physically, mentally and emotionally inferior to men. It was against this backcloth that radical women fought for educational, professional, political and legal rights. Those like Elizabeth, who challenged the traditional views, were often perceived as unattractive troublemakers. Interestingly, we still see shades of this today: a female business leader may be seen as 'bullying,' whilst a male demonstrating similar behaviour is described positively as 'strong'. Perhaps the concept of women and power is one we still struggle with.

♦ ♦ ♦

This was the world in which Elizabeth grew up and from which her beliefs and passions developed. Now it is time to move on, meet her family and look more closely at her young life.

Chapter 2: The young life of a feisty feminist

When she was young, Elizabeth faced personal hardship, disappointment and tragedy. Her sharp brain, inquisitive mind and willingness to speak out emerged early; no doubt they helped to raise her awareness of the suffering of others – but they sometimes got her into trouble.

Despite all she faced, Elizabeth was determined to shape the direction of her life. She must have had a core of steel because her desire for an education and to be a professional woman was a radical stance for a young Victorian girl that brought disapproval and criticism from some of her acquaintances.

Meet the family

Elizabeth's full name was Elizabeth Wolstenholme Elmy Clarke. Wolstenholme was her father's name, Clarke was her mother's maiden name, and Elmy was her lifelong partner and husband.

Her family had its roots firmly in Lancashire, especially in Roe Green, an expanding village on the outskirts of Manchester. From the early 1800s, Roe Green had developed a reputation for uncouth behaviour and drunkenness. In one local guide it was described as:

a god-forgotten place, its inhabitants very much addicted to drink and rude sports, their morals being deplorably low. The whole district is in a state of religious and educational destitution.[1]

Elizabeth's grandparents and her great-grandfather had a strong influence on the village, guiding it from a 'debauched place' to one of fervent religious adherence and temperance (it joined the Temperance Movement in the 1820s).

Samuel Clarke, Elizabeth's great-grandfather, was a religious man who lived and worked in the village. He was distressed by what he perceived as sinful behaviour, and in 1808 he made an invitation that led to the establishment of a local Independent Methodist group. Until 1855, when a chapel opened on the site, preachers stood on a stone to deliver their sermons; this is still visible today in the chapel garden.

Independent Methodism sat outside the mainstream of that denomination; in some ways it was more akin to the Quaker religion, and there were strong links between the two. It emphasised that men and women were equal, and did not accept that the ministry was a profession. Ministers did not get paid, although sometimes they were offered financial support.

Samuel Clarke was key in supporting the growth of this church. By 1816, services and bible classes were occasionally held in his cottage in Lumber Lane. This cottage remained the family home for years; Elizabeth's grandparents (Samuel's son, Richard, and his wife, Mary) lived there. Richard worked hard in the early years of the weaving industry and became a mill owner. Driven by the strong religious beliefs he had learned from his father, and that he shared with his wife, he was widely trusted and respected for his support of others.

Mary Clarke, Elizabeth's grandmother, was an early convert and set up a Sunday school in Roe Green. What remains of her story suggests a caring and generous woman who put others before herself, and for whom religion was an essential part of life. She played a key role in raising funds to build the chapel in Roe Green. It was built on the south-east side of the green where young Elizabeth probably played.

In acknowledging her work to support the building of the chapel, it was written that Mary supported her husband, was kind-hearted and helpful to neighbours. It is interesting that these qualities are the ones that are celebrated, even in a woman who had the strength and determination to successfully run a Sunday school and raise funds to build a chapel. Mary must also have been dedicated and hardworking, traits that her granddaughter inherited. Throughout her life, despite ill health, Elizabeth had the energy and conviction to deliver on her mission.

Elizabeth's parents were Elizabeth (née Clarke) and the Reverend Joseph Wolstenholme. As a minister in the Independent Methodist church, Joseph must have often struggled financially. His bride was twenty-one when they married on 24 December 1828; sadly, her life was cut short in her mid-twenties.

A tough start

Elizabeth had a tough start in the world. She was born on 1 December 1833 in the Cheetham Hill area of Manchester and was baptised on 15 December in Eccles. Throughout her young life, she was surrounded by overcrowded slums as the country forged its way forward with the Industrial Revolution.

In the 1830s, Cheetham Hill teemed with slums. Living conditions for the workers who had moved in to support the cotton and other industries were squalid. Lack of running water and poor sanitation in the overcrowded slums were among the many factors that caused poor health and high mortality rates. The 1832–33 cholera epidemic led to more than 50,000 deaths nationally.

When Elizabeth was born, life expectancy in Manchester was just twenty-six years, and 57% of working-class children died by their fifth birthday. It was not a healthy place for her and thousands of other children.

Everyone in the city, whatever their personal circumstances, must have been aware of the horrors of poverty – unless they chose to turn a blind eye, as many wealthy mill owners did. As the Industrial Revolution took hold in Manchester, Engels and others described it as the vilest and most dangerous of slums.

Elizabeth's parents had three children: Joseph was born in 1829 and went on to become a famous mathematician; Richard, born in 1831, died aged nine, and Elizabeth. Terrible misfortune befell her at birth; within three days her mother died, and she was placed in foster care in the nearby village of Walkden.

Walkden, like Roe Green, was on the Duke of Bridgewater's estate. The third Duke (1736–1803) was certainly open to change and saw the potential for expanding markets as the Industrial Revolution began. He recognised the need for better transport to exploit the open coal seams on his estate in Worsley and instigated the construction of the first true British canal from Worsley to Manchester and Salford. Thousands of tonnes of coal and other materials passed along it; no doubt young Elizabeth saw the barges coming and going, and possibly talked to folk working on the canal.

After three years in foster care, Elizabeth returned to her father after he remarried. His new wife was Mary Lord, the daughter of a woollen manufacturer, who could support a stable and reasonably comfortable family life. That stability did not last long; as a minister, Joseph's profession was itinerant, and they moved to Sunderland, probably in 1837.

They lived there for four years before returning to Roe Green in 1841 because of Joseph's deteriorating health. It is likely that from then until her father's death in 1845 Elizabeth was largely responsible for caring for him. Poor living conditions and a lack of healthcare meant that illness and death were never far from one's door.

The family moved to a house near Elizabeth's grandparents in Lumber Lane. Like Walkden, Roe Green was the site of coal mining, cotton mills and heavy ironworks. In 1841 the records show only two non-manual workers in Roe Green: Richard Clarke (Elizabeth's grandfather, who was a cotton mill owner) and his son-in-law, the Reverend Joseph Wolstenholme (Elizabeth's father).

Despite the growth of work in the mills, Roe Green still had a high proportion of handloom weavers. As this group was predominant in the Peterloo Massacre, young Elizabeth will have heard eyewitness reports, or at least been told stories handed down by families involved in the tragedy that played out that day.

While serving as a minister in Roe Green, Joseph Wolstenholme stood on the stone in the churchyard many times to deliver a sermon and Elizabeth must have stood in all weathers to listen to him. She would also have attended her grandmother's Sunday school. It seems that grandmother and granddaughter had a warm relationship because Elizabeth kept returning to Lumber Lane until Mary's death in 1857.

Together with her family and neighbours, Elizabeth enjoyed a day out to celebrate Queen Victoria's coronation in 1837. As she watched the procession in Rochdale, she was held by the daughter of John Petrie, one of many in her family network who were to influence her understanding of radical views.

The Queen did not visit the Manchester area until 1851 because of its frequent political rallies and radical politics. However, when she *did* visit, Rochdale Town Hall was fitted out to ensure her comfort: a single lavatory was built especially for her.[*]

As Elizabeth grew up, her inquisitive mind sometimes led her into trouble. On one occasion, she questioned her father about the religious doctrine of eternal punishment. A female questioning her father and her religion would have been regarded as highly inappropriate. Although she may have wanted to learn by engaging in dialogue, her father was outraged

---

[*] Rochdale Town Hall is currently closed for refurbishment; planned to re-open in 2023.

and she received a severe thrashing. This was to be the first of many events that led her to denounce religion.

There were many occasions when her inquisitive mind was engaged and dialogue flowed around her. The whole family would have been influenced by Richard Clarke's radical liberal views, and consequently were strongly connected with many local and national figures who encouraged Elizabeth's political awareness. These included John Bright* and Richard Cobden, who worked together in 1838 to establish the Anti-Corn Law League.

John Bright was born in Rochdale in 1811 to a Quaker family. During his visits to Lumber Lane, he may have introduced Elizabeth to pacifism, humanitarianism and feminist ideals – heady stuff for an inquisitive young girl. Bright was a Rochdale mill owner and Liberal MP for Manchester between 1847 and 1857; as well as playing a leading role in abolishing the Corn Laws, he was also famous for his anti-slavery stance. Richard Cobden moved to Lancashire and in 1831 opened a calico printing mill; as part of the Corn Law fight, he became an MP in 1841.

Elizabeth's mind was developing at a time when the Corn Laws were causing great anger and distress among the northern radicals. The Corn Laws, also known as the Bread Tax, had been introduced in 1815 to protect British producers of wheat and maize and had resulted in higher prices for bread.

In 1838, the ongoing challenge to these laws resulted in the establishment of the Anti-Corn Law League (ACLL).

---

* As an adult, Elizabeth worked closely with John's younger brother, Jacob. Unlike Jacob, John was a radical but against female emancipation.

Eight years of campaigning followed, and many meetings were held in Manchester and beyond to argue for the repeal of the laws. To accommodate the large numbers that attended these meetings, the League constructed a temporary pavilion because no other site in Manchester could hold the crowds. They went on to make the pavilion permanent and, once the laws were repealed, constructed a building on the site. The Free Trade Hall is a fine memorial to the battles these free traders fought to reduce the price of bread for those living under the constant threat of hunger and starvation.

In September 1843, as part of the fight for the repeal of the laws, *The Economist* was founded to voice the arguments for free trade. Publications the length and breadth of the country printed articles debating and reporting on this issue; it was one of the hot topics of the time and rarely out of the headlines. Events were held across the country and, considering how engaged her family were with the radical politics of the day, it is likely that Elizabeth attended some of those in Manchester.

In 1841, women supporters of the ACLL held a bazaar in Manchester. Many years later, Jacob Bright (John Bright's brother) reminded people at a suffrage event that the bazaar had been of a 'prodigious size', and that the women had sold a whole range of merchandise. This one event raised about £10,000, a huge sum at that time.

A few years later, the *Manchester Times* reported a meeting of free traders in the city on 13 December 1845, highlighting the excitement in the preceding days as the public clamoured to get tickets. The speakers included both Bright and Cobden; talk was of the 'uphill agitation', and how finally they were hopeful of achieving their aims.

In February 1846, many newspapers carried a call from the council of the ACLL for the friends of free trade to start petitions calling for the immediate abolition of the Corn Laws. Interestingly, Elizabeth frequently used petitions to the government to raise issues with politicians; perhaps this was an early lesson for her in the importance of influencing those with power and getting politicians (all men, of course) on side.

The Corn Laws were finally repealed in August 1846, and Elizabeth attended the celebrations in Manchester to cheer the success of the free traders. At the age of twelve, she identified these events as the start of her political consciousness. Not only had her conscience been woken, but she had also learned vital lessons about engaging people and carrying through difficult campaigns.

During this period Elizabeth was caring for her father, whose health continued to decline until he died in August 1845. Being a carer and witnessing her father's death must have been physically, mentally and emotionally hard for such a young girl.

The laws of the time did not allow her stepmother, Mary, to become Elizabeth's guardian so she was given into the care of her maternal family, the Clarkes. The deaths of her mother and her father must have been significant for Elizabeth, influencing her fight for women to gain custody of their children.

Her grandfather, Richard Clarke, played a significant role in the direction of Elizabeth's young life by agreeing to fund her education at Fulneck Moravian School near Pudsey, Leeds. She was keen to continue her education, and the

Moravian schools endeavoured to provide girls with a more robust curriculum than was typical for girls at the time.

Off to school

Going to school was the second time that Elizabeth moved away from Lancashire. She faced an arduous journey across the Pennines. The train service linking Manchester and Leeds did not start until late October 1848, so she would have travelled across the southern Pennines to Wakefield on a turnpike road that had been improved in 1839. It ran through Marsden and offered good views of the Leeds–Liverpool Canal, a feature that would become familiar to Elizabeth as she repeated the journey over the next two years.

Established in the 1740s, there is still a school at the Fulneck Moravian settlement. Education is very important to Moravians and they have a reputation for giving a sound education of the type that Elizabeth wished to pursue. But why was she, a Methodist, sent to a Moravian School – and why one in Yorkshire?

During the 1800s there were strong links between Methodists, the Moravians and the Quakers. There was, and still is, a Moravian settlement at Fairfield, about twelve miles from Roe Green, so there was probably contact between these two religious communities.

Richard Clarke may have had business contacts in Leeds and been sympathetic to the politics of the area; Leeds was also a centre of working-class radicalism and had a well-established Chartist movement. In 1848, Leeds was hit by cholera like other northern towns, but this did not deter Elizabeth's move to the school, possibly because the disease took a heavy toll in the poorer, crowded parts of Leeds. Fulneck, despite its proximity to the increasingly industrialised area of Pudsey, was set amid agricultural land and was still relatively healthy.

Fulneck is still a Moravian settlement. It was completed in 1746 and there have been only a few significant additions since then, so Elizabeth would recognise the settlement today. It is built on the side of Tong Valley, and she would have been familiar with the houses, school, church and the beautiful views across the local countryside.

The church where Moravians have worshipped for centuries is at the centre of the settlement both literally and metaphorically. No doubt schoolchildren heard the stories of the founder of the Moravian faith, Count Zinzendorf, who provided a home on his land in Germany for religious refugees in the 1620s. Stories of his visits to the Fulneck settlement were shared with great pride; the children must have enjoyed the trumpet being blown from the Bell Tower on top of the church to announce the arrival of such an important guest. Elizabeth will have heard it when highly regarded guests came, and also to mark funerals.

By the 1840s, the settlement comprised a shop, a bakery and an inn; the latter became the Temperance Hotel in 1847, which brought it in line with the temperance views of Roe Green and Elizabeth's family on the evils of drink. In her day, the shop supplied exercise books; today the same building is a café frequented by pupils and staff.

The school had an embroidery business run by sixteen needlewomen and seamstresses[*]. Although it had gone

---

[*] Numbers from the 1851 census.

through hard times, by the 1840s it was flourishing and regular orders were despatched every month to London. Pupils will have seen the progress of the work on a cushion that was presented to Queen Victoria and Prince Albert then placed in the Great Exhibition of 1851.

Embroidery may have been new to Elizabeth but other sights were familiar, such as the mill above the settlement for grinding locally grown corn (at the top of the imaginatively titled Mill Hill), and the coal carts that paid a toll of tuppence to pass through Fulneck to the Bankhouse Mill. Some of the local men and women worked in the woollen mills in Pudsey, just a short walk away.

The school was well-established by the time Elizabeth arrived, having opened soon after the creation of the settlement. There was also a boys' school, although they lived and were taught separately and only joined the girls for daily worship.

Education was (and continues to be) a key element of the Moravian Church, based upon writings of the highly influential Moravian philosopher Jan Amos Comenius, who placed the welfare of humanity at the centre of his work. He developed and applied a child-centred system of education, believing that children would learn more effectively if their education was enjoyable, varied and involved pictures. Consequently, Elizabeth experienced a very different approach to the rote learning of her early years. As she went on to play a key role in Victorian education, we can assume that her experiences at Fulneck were significant to her future work.

It is amazing to reflect that Elizabeth went into a church that is still in regular use. The main difference to the building is that the benches have been replaced by pews, but the four large windows that look out over Tong Valley still fill the church with light whenever the sun shines. In Elizabeth's time they were plain glass,* but they were replaced in 1933. In addition to glorious views, the windows brought warmth to the students, especially on cold winter's mornings; there was no central heating in those days!

The school day started at 6.00am, breakfast was at 7.00am and then lessons. These included English, arithmetic, geography, history and natural history. Records show that the school purchased a second-hand pianoforte in 1818; perhaps Elizabeth used this (or a newer one) when she had music lessons. School records also show that her family paid additional money for her to have language lessons; no doubt these were part of her determination to gain the best education she could.

The 1841 census shows that the school had forty-nine pupils and six teachers. Pupil ages ranged from six to fifteen, with more than half being between thirteen and fifteen. Almost all the younger children were the children of Moravian ministers serving abroad and had been born in the West Indies or Ireland. Elizabeth encountered some well-travelled children, although most of the older pupils were born in this country and were fee paying.

The girls' school was below the church, so sometimes the organ was clearly audible. As well as attending regular services, the pupils went to special services for five of the

---

* The church is built on a hill. The entrance is at the back and the windows are all at the front on the second floor above the terrace. They all look across Tong Valley.

Moravian Memorial days.* These were accompanied by a band and the choral groups; music is highly valued by Moravians and an integral part of their worship.

At Easter, the pupils sang 'The Children's Hosanna' on Palm Sunday. The following Sunday, a trumpet sounded at 4.00am and they paraded down to God's Acre** to celebrate Easter Sunday as the sun rose over the fields, a tradition that continues today – although the service is now at 7.00am.

Like all pupils at Fulneck, Elizabeth will have learned the principles of the Moravian faith, so it is worth taking a brief look at them and considering how they may have contributed to the way she lived her life.

Fellowship: togetherness focusing on equality and bridging social differences. Elizabeth was passionate about fairness for all.

Ideal of Service: to feel and live in service to others. Her life was dedicated to working for female equality.

Simplicity: to focus on complicated relations of things and identify clear facts. This was an important skill for her work as an advisor on government papers. She became the first paid secretary for the Personal Rights Association (PRA), set up in 1871, to ensure all legislation guarded personal and human rights.

Happiness: a warmth and joy in how a life is lived. Elizabeth had thousands of connections worldwide, which she maintained through her correspondence, and a partner, Ben, who was the love of her life.[2]

---

* There are six Memorial Days but as one falls during August the pupils will have been on holiday.

** This is the title given to all Moravian burial grounds.

Life after Fulneck

The Fulneck records show that Elizabeth was academically very able in addition to her abilities in music and languages. Despite this, her family dealt her a significant injustice by refusing to fund the continuation of her education. She had a strong desire to learn and throughout her life she believed firmly in continuing personal development. Her uncle pleaded with her to confine herself to what was socially acceptable for a young woman, but Elizabeth regarded such a role as useless. It was not what she envisaged for her life.

Elizabeth wished to attend the recently established Bedford College for Women but her guardians rejected this, despite supporting her older brother in his academic studies. To enable him to join a profession, he completed a master's degree in 1852 then studied at Christ's College, Cambridge; his education certainly was of value as he went on to become a brilliant mathematician. This must have been a blow for his sister, and one of the many injustices that fired her passion to fight for education for girls and women.

Had her guardians agreed to her attending Bedford College, she would have been studying alongside women with whom she later worked in her many campaigns. These included Barbara Leigh Smith (later Bodichon), who became a campaigner for women's property rights and founded Girton College, Cambridge, and Bessie Rayner Parkes, a campaigner for equal opportunities for women in education and employment.

Showing her strength of character, Elizabeth refused to be defeated. Between 1850 and 1852, she undertook the difficult route of independent study. The Open University did not come into existence until more than a century later so, with quiet determination, she read economics, politics, case law and Latin. This enabled her to apply successfully for the role of governess in a household in Luton.

Working as a governess

As the affluent middle class became more status conscious and established a comfortable lifestyle, having a governess to teach one's children was recognised as a mark of social 'arrival'. The role was valued; however, the governess herself was often in a difficult position within the household.

> *I think the phrase that really sums up the governess is betwixt and between. She's a woman who's employed to look after somebody else's children, but she doesn't have children herself. She's a genteel lady, but the family that employs her doesn't really think that she's smart enough to sit down to dinner with them. And the servants, who wait on her, think really that she's no better than them and they really can't stand her stuck up airs. She's supposed to dress appropriately, which means elegantly, but she doesn't actually have enough money really to get her boots repaired or to get her gloves cleaned. I mean, she's in the middle of a kind of lot of, lot of tensions, and living them out must have been an incredibly uncomfortable situation in which to be.*[3]

Elizabeth headed south to Luton, Bedfordshire. Had she read some novels of the period, she might have appreciated the life into which she was moving.

Her broad education at Fulneck, plus her independent studies, were useful because the role of the governess was varied depending upon the ages and number of children in the family. Teaching basic literacy and numeracy were the foundation, after which boys were sent to boarding school. Girls stayed at home and received some training in languages (usually French) and geography. Older girls were offered drawing and piano lessons.

Mothers considered dancing and deportment important. Many of them regarded education for girls as having the sole aim of ensuring that their daughters attracted a suitable husband and saw off the competition. Considering her views, it is doubtful if this aim sat comfortably with Elizabeth. However, living with a middle-class family offered her an insight into a social class with which she had previously had little direct contact. She gained an appreciation of how they lived their lives, the role of the wife in maintaining the home for her husband, and the experiences of women working as servants.

Back to Roe Green

In 1854, Elizabeth headed north back to Roe Green. By this time her grandfather had died, and it may have been an inheritance from him that enabled her to establish her first school at Boothstown Road in Worsley. Interestingly, the same uncle who had prevented her continuing her formal education after Fulneck had changed his view and proved supportive of her first school. Perhaps this is one of many examples in her life of how Elizabeth's commitment to her beliefs and sheer determination to follow them through gained her respect and influenced the opinions of others.

She worked full time as a headmistress until her stance on religion drove her to leave teaching in 1871.

Elizabeth and religion

As we have already discussed, Elizabeth grew up with people for whom religion was a fundamental part of how they lived their lives. Initially this was with her family, for whom Independent Methodism was an active part of each day, then she had two years at a school where church attendance was integral to the daily routine. When she was first employed, it was at a time when many middle-class families wanted a governess to include religious teaching and prayers for their children.

Elizabeth's sharp mind had always driven her to question religion. We have already seen how questioning her father had resulted in severe physical punishment. Later in her life, even the wedding of her brother, Joseph, to whom she was close, would not tempt her into a church to hear the bride say she would obey her husband. This, and other such injustices, turned a girl who was naturally questioning into a firm nonbeliever.

Joseph had some experiences in common with her, yet he remained an active Christian and became a priest in the Church of England. For him, this sat comfortably alongside his scepticism, and he will have introduced her to other sceptics, thus enabling her to discuss her views openly. The Secularist Societies founded in the 1840s were based upon the principles of equality and free inquiry, both of which were close to Elizabeth's heart.

Many factors informed the development of secularist opinion, particularly the philosophical shift associated with the Enlightenment, the growth of scientific understanding and expanding urbanisation. Secularisation in nineteenth-century Britain was primarily a political process in which the state slowly relinquished its jurisdiction over the religious beliefs of citizens. However, during much of Elizabeth's life, a refusal to accept religious principles could be a significant obstacle to involvement in education and civic participation.

Victorian feminists grappled with what they perceived to be a contradiction in religion as it was set out each Sunday from the pulpit, a contradiction that was frequently discussed in the literature of the 1830s and 1840s. Religion, together with much of society, saw women as subordinate to men, yet often they were placed as the spiritual lead within the home.

Many feminists struggled with this dilemma, especially the religious view of women as subservient; some accepted it, while others turned from organised religion. Frances Power Cobbe, for example, was excluded from the family home for refusing to attend family prayers. In common with some of those with whom she worked during her campaigns, religion played no positive part in Elizabeth's life as moved into adulthood.

Influences on young Elizabeth

Family life, the place we grow up, what is happening in the world around us, our education, what we read and who we listen to all have an impact on who we become and what we believe. Before examining Elizabeth's many campaigns, it is useful to take a brief look at some of the influences on this young, emerging feminist.

The Poor Law drove many of the desperately poor into the workhouses, and Elizabeth grew up in the shadow of one such place. Throughout her childhood it was visible on the horizon, overshadowing the lives of all around her. She must have witnessed the desperation of people who tried to avoid ending up at its door.

We have already considered the gossip and the debates that will have swirled around Elizabeth. As an inquisitive, intelligent child she read widely, and this also informed her views as they emerged.

If feminism and the movement for women's rights had a founding text, many consider it to be *A Vindication of the Rights of Woman* by Mary Wollstonecraft. Not all Victorian feminists subscribed to its views, but Elizabeth read it and saw it as playing a key role in developing her understanding of women's rights.

Mary Wollstonecraft had an unhappy childhood and suffered abuse at the hands of her violent father; she went on to write books that challenged the position of women and how they viewed themselves. In 1792, she published her response to Edmund Burke's *Reflections on the French Revolution* (published in 1790) and Thomas Paine's *Rights of Man* (1791). Stirred by the liberating principles underpinning the French Revolution, Burke and Paine argued for the rights of man; Mary Wollstonecraft argued for the rights of women to be equal to those of men. In terms of education and of equality, this must have aligned with the emerging views of young Elizabeth.

The education of women has, of late, been more
attended to than formerly; yet they are still reckoned as a
frivolous sex, and ridiculed or pitied by the writers who
endeavour by satire or instruction to improve them. It is
acknowledged that they spend many of the fifty years of
their lives in acquiring a smattering of accomplishments:
meanwhile strength of body and mind are sacrificed to
libertine notions of beauty, to the desire of establishing
themselves, ... the only way women can rise in the world,
by marriage.[4]

Towards the end of her book, Wollstonecraft argues
strongly for the rights of women, proposing that when
women are seen as equal they will emulate the virtues of
men and will *grow more perfect when emancipated* (page
451).

Elizabeth not only read books but will have absorbed
newspapers, as they presented world affairs in ways that
informed her thinking. For example, in the months before
she left for Fulneck revolution was once more stalking
Europe, resulting in radical articles appearing in many
newspapers.

This still small voice of truth which sounds the undertone
in the storm and whirlwind of these human passions, in
the discordant crash of falling thrones and dynasties,
may be thus interpreted – that the conventional shall
no longer stand securely against the real, no not though
supported by countless soldiers, and all the appliances
of modern warfare. If there is meaning and significance
in this French Revolution it is this, first and principally
– that the best laid devices, planned and executed by
the craftiest and wisest, will certainly fail in western

Europe to destroy the political liberty of the people. The French Revolution of 1848 illustrates the pretty generally recognised truth - that kings and governments are now organs by which the popular will and intelligence exerts and manifests itself. This being the case, to train and invigorate the popular intelligence, to pervade it with the principles of the purest morality, so that the popular may be rationally directed to the highest aims and purposes, is now the mission and the field of the true reformer.[5]

This could read as a call to arms to all reformers at the time and was quite possibly inspiring for young Elizabeth.

Interestingly, the article starts by bemoaning the slow pace of weekly journalists in responding to the new technology of electric telegraphs and railways that could provide more current news. The writer believed that the latest news in the weeklies was flat and stale. This is another example of the changing world in which Elizabeth was growing up; she recognised the importance of keeping in touch with the public as she assumed a more political stance.

While Elizabeth was working as a governess in 1852, Elizabeth Cleghorn Gaskell published the novel *Ruth*. Gaskell, also from Manchester, had published her first novel in 1848. Entitled *Mary Barton*, its subtitle *A Tale of Manchester Life* may well have appealed to Elizabeth. *Mary Barton* had a great impact on the reading public and was widely reviewed and discussed. Its subject matter – the appalling state of the poor in the Manchester area – awakened the nation's conscience and aligned closely with Elizabeth's personal experiences.

Ruth focused upon the hardships of a young female apprentice and the sharp division between the rich and the poor. It illustrated how some wealthy people felt able to use and abuse the poor without any thought. In the story, Ruth has been orphaned and works long hours into the night as an apprentice to a dressmaker, with many clients among local upper-class women. While at a county ball, mending dresses torn during the dancing, a young aristocrat notices her beauty. Her life of drudgery and emptiness is filled by the attentions of this young man – but naturally he abandons her when she becomes pregnant. The book offers a rich description of Ruth's desperate situation and the dilemmas she faces; it will have resonated with Elizabeth, and once again stirred her anger at the position of women.

Growing up in Manchester exposed Elizabeth to hardships in a radically changing world. Being female, she was one of the oppressed half of the population who received an inadequate education. However, her determination, her inquisitive mind, education and reading opened her to the emerging views calling for a seismic shift in how women were seen and their role in society.

By the time she returned to Roe Green, her life had been touched by poor health and death. She had lived alongside poverty and witnessed first-hand the injustices women suffered. She had also dedicated herself to hard work to gain an education. Here lies the foundation for a passionate, energetic young woman to step into the role of campaigner and feminist.

Chapter 3: The three 'Es'

Like Tony Blair, Elizabeth could have used the rallying call of 'education, education, education'. She was passionate about education for herself, for all girls, and for teachers.

Equally, for her the three Es could have stood for education, employment and empowerment. As a young person she fought for an education so that she could gain employment and be empowered to live life as she chose, something that she also fought for on behalf of all women.

Elizabeth became a highly respected headmistress and argued that the standard of education for girls should be raised. By playing a key role in a growing network of like-minded women, she placed herself at the centre of the push for change.

Such change rarely comes easily. There were strong, practical arguments for it, yet the entrenched views against change were hard to overcome, particularly as the power to bring about change was largely held by men.

The arguments were debated and set out in various publications. Elizabeth wrote with clarity and passion about the need for women to have employment supported by a sound education, and her work was instrumental in opening up educational opportunities. Educated women sought out better employment and gradually prejudices diminished, though they did not disappear.

What was the education system like for women at the time, and how did it gradually change?

An overview of education

Between 1800 and 1900 there was a huge increase in literacy across the population. In 1800, only 60% of men and 40% of women were literate; by 1900, this was approximately 90% for both.

As the world became more complex and employers required literate employees, illiteracy was acknowledged as a serious problem. Not being able to read or write was equivalent to being unable to use technology and social media today. Many writers highlighted the problem; Charles Dickens, one of the most influential, exposed the rates of illiteracy and expounded the view that improving them was vital to empowering people of all classes.

Education was divided by class in a rigidly stratified society. Working-class children employed in factories had a legal right from 1844 to schooling for six half-days a week; this followed the 1833 Factory Act, which mandated two hours education a day. The 1870 Education Act was a major driver in improving literacy rates as it provided for all children to attend elementary education; however, there were still many barriers to attendance such as parents having to pay for exercise books.

Sunday Schools and Ragged Schools provided some education, particularly for children from very poor families. Ragged Schools were started in 1818 and by 1870 there were about 350 of them across the country. Teaching methods were generally not engaging, rote learning was common, and so was the practice of brighter children teaching the young ones.

Initially little attention was given to the education of middle-class children who were taught at home by a governess. Older boys went to boarding school, while the governess focused on teaching girls the accomplishments a wife required. Until nearly 1850 there was no provision for ensuring governesses themselves received a broad education. Although Elizabeth was determined to pursue her education despite the lack of family support, not all governesses were motivated to undertake personal study.

Standards of teaching within schools varied greatly but they shared a common factor: girls' needs were subservient to boys'. It was into this situation that women stepped to demand good quality education for girls and recognised standards for teacher training.

From Sunday Schools through to universities, education was closely aligned to religion; in fact, until the University Test Act was passed in 1871, Cambridge and Oxford students and academics had to be practising members of the Church of England. Sadly for the pupils in Congleton, this was the year that Elizabeth stood down from teaching because of her secular views. However, she continued to play a vital role in improving education provision for both girls and for teachers.

The arguments for education and employment were interrelated and often presented alongside each other in pamphlets and texts.

Education: the arguments for

The arguments for a high-quality education for girls and openings into higher education were philosophical, social and economic. As with many other issues during this period, they were also frequently along class lines.

The Victorian women arguing for education were building on the work of earlier campaigners. As early as the seventeenth century, Mary Astell (who was born in 1666) used different philosophical ideas to argue that women should receive a higher education and to undermine the belief that women were naturally intellectually inferior to men. Many years later, Mary Wollstonecraft set up a school to encourage her radical views and spoke regularly about the importance of education for women.

Elizabeth and her colleague Josephine Butler saw education as fundamental to removing female oppression; they both equated education with a freedom that would come from gaining knowledge. The topic was discussed regularly in the *English Women's Journal*, established in 1858 by Barbara Bodichon (nee Leigh Smith), who clearly stated that women needed an education in order to improve society.

Feminists such as Elizabeth, Josephine Butler and Barbara Bodichon believed that the enforced idleness of middle-class women was both a sin and an insult to their dignity. They regarded the financial dependence forced upon women when they married as wrong. They argued that freedom of knowledge and the opportunity for economic gain should replace ignorance and idleness.

The church held great sway over public opinion. Some

denominations argued that women were equal to men in the eyes of God. Belief in equality and education for all was fundamental to the Moravian Church, and, in the early 1800s, the Unitarians rejected the concept of original sin and argued strongly for a woman's right to education. Interestingly, as a young child it was about original sin that Elizabeth had questioned her father – and received a beating. However, unlike Elizabeth, some Victorian feminists (including Josephine Butler and Barbara Bodichon) remained aligned to the church and insisted that women's education was compatible with Christian teachings.

These women fighting for the right to an education for girls and women were skilled polemicists and didn't shy away from contentious issues. In 1869, when Josephine Butler edited *Woman's Work and Woman's Culture*,[1] she invited Elizabeth to contribute a chapter on education.

Elizabeth started by acknowledging that they were on the eve of great educational reforms as a significant Education Bill was passing through the House of Commons. However, she immediately weighed in saying how vital this was because, rather than being first among European countries in education, as many believed: *we are so far fallen behind in the onward march of other nations that it is now the special shame of England to possess almost the worst instructed people in Europe.* (p. 290) It was a strong opening statement that she followed with more radical views.

She highlighted the emphasis placed upon for the middle-class boys' education and argued that the needs of working-class children were equally important. She made it clear that gendered characteristics, which typically painted

51

women as intellectually inferior, were social constructs that could be eradicated.

Regarding equality, she stated that:

we are not one nation of Englishmen and another nation of Englishwomen, but one nation of English men and women, and that, as a matter of the soundest national policy and a means of the highest social well-being, it is imperative that Englishwomen should be as well instructed as Englishmen. (p. 294)

She lamented that many middle-class girls were taught mostly at home because their parents were apathetic about their education. Too much emphasis was placed upon accomplishments to prepare them for a good marriage; these, according to Elizabeth, were a waste of energy and brain power that could benefit the individual and society.

As part of her questioning of gender differences and the need to achieve a sound education for all, Elizabeth drew on contemporary research to argue the benefits of mixed education. Having read a report of an experiment conducted in Liverpool in 1868 by the Rev. G Butler (yes, Josephine's husband), she stated that mixed classes were both feasible and realistic.

the only objections to such an experiment rest on moral and social grounds. Why should it be considered so dangerous and doubtful for boys and girls or for men and women to share each other's serious pursuits whilst they are allowed freely to share each other's frivolities...

(p. 326)

She concluded by flagging up the issue of higher education for women.

But whatever solution of present difficulties may be

found, it is plain that the question of the higher education of women is a most urgent one, one which will not bear to be delayed. We plead the cause of women. We ask that the gifts of God may not be wasted, that women themselves may not be robbed of some of the purest joys of life, those of intellectual effort and achievement, and that society which needs their help so much may not be defrauded of their best and worthiest service. Give us knowledge, power, and life. We will repay that gift a hundred-fold. Set free the women who sigh in the dark prison-houses, the captives of ignorance and folly. Cruel tyrants are these; slay them! With yourselves, people of England, it rests to put an end to that frivolity of which you say you are so weary. Help women to become wise, that they may be just, true, merciful and loving. (pp. 327–328)

Elizabeth fully appreciated the power of the pen. She could present a balanced, rational argument, draw upon research, use the views of others and employ emotive phrases to stir up positive responses to stimulate debate and action.

Education: the arguments against

The Enlightenment had accelerated the call for education for women but had also provoked hostile reactions. For example, in *Emile*, published in 1762, Rousseau stated clearly that a woman's function is purely to please men and they only need to learn domestic skills. These views were still very much in evidence in Victorian England where women were literally and metaphorically invisible. Working-class women could be seen in the fields, mills and in domestic service, but they were always under the control of men, be that their father, husband or employer. Middle-class women were largely hidden away in their homes, living according to the principles of a patriarchal society.

Middle-class women in particular operated in a separate sphere to men, and many people regarded education as a threat to these spheres and to family life. In 1839 Sarah Stickney Ellis[2] wrote about the duties of the women, making it clear that they must accept the superiority of a husband, who must always be treated with respect and deference. Education for girls was purely to prepare them for a good marriage and to equip them to please their husbands.

Even a group of intellectual women known as the Bluestockings, who met to share learning and debate issues, generally subscribed to the popular view that women should be submissive and only maintain a role in the domestic sphere.

Neither did the medical profession help the cause with some doctors suggesting education could damage girls' mental and physical development and make them sterile! Other doctors argued that education was wasted on women because their brains were significantly smaller than men's and inferior.

Not all women who contributed to the education of girls aligned themselves with women's rights. Some reputable headmistresses of girls' schools were opposed to female enfranchisement.

Changing the face of education

The 1851 census identified 67,551 women teachers. Like Elizabeth, many had undertaken their education through self-directed study, Sunday school teaching and by attending public lectures. Many of them were becoming interested in developing teaching as a profession; consequently, Elizabeth had the chance to turn her vision into reality by becoming highly influential during an important era for women's education.

Indicative of the changes that were taking place is the 1861 census, in which the category for teaching was changed from a 'learned occupation' to 'profession'. Elizabeth, like many of her colleagues, was keen for education to be recognised as a profession; in addition to being based upon qualifications and recognition, this implied intellectual ability, modernity and efficiency.

One of the moves towards modernity was the exploration of a child-centred approach to education, partly driven by a resistance to rote learning and the many tests used for educating boys. In 1854, Sarah Jolly wrote about the importance of understanding individual pupils and developing an awareness of how each child approached learning.[3] Having been exposed to the Moravian approach to teaching at Fulneck School, which is based on the work of Jan Comenius who firmly espoused enjoyment and engagement as vital for learning, such ideas will have appealed to Elizabeth.

She fulfilled her wish to become an independent, educated, professional woman. During the 1860s in Worsley, Manchester, she became one of the country's foremost headmistresses. She founded a school at Moody Hall, Congleton in 1867, where she served as headmistress until 1871. Whilst working tirelessly as a full-time headmistress, she was also driving forward the cause of women's education and employment as she strove to make what she had achieved more accessible to others.

She wrote *The Education for Girls* (1869) partly in response to the Schools Enquiry Commission (Taunton Commission) set up in the mid-1860s to investigate educational provision for the middle classes. Initially the commission's arguments related to the role of men in society and focused on how education should enable a man to earn a living and develop a sense of personal awareness.

Elizabeth challenged this vigorously. Through the work of another Victorian feminist, Emily Davies, the commission extended its remit to include the education of girls and called Elizabeth to present evidence. On 19 April 1866, Elizabeth became the first woman to testify to a Royal Commission; she was indeed stepping into a man's world. Although this was a situation in which many of us would have been overawed, she spoke clearly about the value and importance of a sound education for all.

She may well have been summoned by the commission because of the impact she had when she joined the College of Preceptors in 1862. The college was established in 1846 to: *promote sound learning and advancing the interests of education ... affording facilities to the teacher for acquiring sound knowledge of the profession.*[4]

It was a forum that contributed to the development of teaching as a profession and it became increasingly significant for women teachers. The college, and subsequently its regional groups, campaigned for the registration and certification of teachers. This significantly improved the pupils' experience of school and teaching standards.

When she joined the college, Elizabeth was dismayed by the standard of elementary education for girls. She met many people who shared her views, who believed that women's oppression in all aspects of life was related to their intellectual oppression. They vigorously challenged the view set out by writers such as Sara Ellis that daughters and wives of middle-class men were inferior mentally and in all other ways to their men and should be content to undertake philanthropy.

Elizabeth met Emily Davies through the College of Preceptors. Together they went on to establish one of its regional associations, the Manchester Schoolmistresses' Association, in 1865. These associations fostered a growing sense of identity and professional authority; their approach was based upon the principles of collaboration and reciprocity. The members were keen to share ideas and good practice, which led to strong links across the regions.

Led by Elizabeth and Emily, the Manchester Schoolmistresses' Association promoted access to university examinations to raise the standard of education for girls. Together with others, they spent a few weeks collecting signatures from 900 teachers of girls;[5] the petition was submitted to the Senate of Cambridge University, which consequently accepted that girls could enter local examinations. In December 1865, Elizabeth accompanied twenty-one girls for their first exams – and all of them were successful.

The following year one of her former male pupils, the vicar of Worsley, wrote an article in the *Daily News* praising Elizabeth's contribution in equipping her pupils with skills that enabled them to go on to productive employment. Worsley became the external examiner of the Grange School in Congleton and supported Elizabeth's work to get teachers accredited.

Attention was also on higher education that would allow females over eighteen to gain qualifications, as this was often the route into employment. The Schoolmistresses' Associations joined forces to create the North of England Council for Promoting the Higher Education of Women. Inspired by Anne Clough, its first meeting was held in Leeds in November 1867. Elizabeth represented the Manchester Association and played a key role of drawing up the rules of the new body.

The council organised a series of lectures and was active in challenging the refusal of universities to open their examinations to women. Elizabeth, among others, wrote to many newspapers as part of a strategy to put pressure on the university senates.

The following appeared in the Leeds Mercury on Thursday 28 May 1868.

The Vice-Chancellor of Cambridge has received the following important memorials:

1.   To the Vice-Chancellor and the Senate of the University of Cambridge. Gentlemen, – We, the undersigned, being either connected with or engaged in the education of girls, desire to bring under your consideration the great want which is felt by women of the upper and middle classes, particularly those engaged in teaching, of higher examinations, suitable to their own needs. The local examinations, to which, by a grace of the senate passed in April 1865, girls under eighteen have now for three years been admitted, have proved of the greatest advantage in stimulating and steadying the work in girls' schools. Students above eighteen are not, however, admissible to these examinations, nor are they of a sufficiently advanced character to meet the wants of such students, especially of those who have adopted, or wish to adopt, teaching as a profession. We therefore beg that, taking into consideration the grave necessities of the case, you will be pleased, either by extending the powers of the syndicate for conducting local examinations, or in some other way, to make provision for such examinations as shall adequately test and attest the higher education of women. – We are, gentlemen, your obedient servants.

(Signed) Josephine E. Butler, President of the North of England Council for Higher Education of Women; Anne J. Clough, Secretary of the North of England Council for Promoting Higher Education of Women; Elizabeth Gwyn, President of the Manchester Board of Schoolmistresses and Representative: Elizabeth C. Wolstenholme, Representative of the Manchester Board of Schoolmistresses.[6]

They got the result they wanted: by October 1868, Cambridge University had agreed to award a diploma, thus providing the first professional accreditation for women educators. It was these steps that contributed to the establishment of Newnham College, Cambridge.

Newnham College opened in 1871 as a house for five students in Regent Street, Cambridge, where they could live while attending lectures. Anne Clough was in charge of these students. On its website, Newnham College describes itself today as a: *lively and sociable women's College at the heart of the University of Cambridge. Founded in 1871, we are the oldest College run by women. For women.*[7]

Throughout the 1860s, Elizabeth made a significant contribution to the development of the education system. How the world has changed thanks to the hard work and determination of women such as her; today, approximately 60% of students entering higher education are female.

Employment: for and against

Like Elizabeth, Josephine Butler clearly connected the issues of education and employment. In 1868, she wrote:

> *The desire for education which is widely felt by English women ... springs ... from the conviction that for many women to get knowledge is the only way to get bread.*[8]

Although Emily Davies was not in favour of the vote for women, she was keen on employment for women and believed that they could enter business, train as doctors, hospital and prison managers. However, like so many campaigners, in her writing she acknowledged the dilemmas women faced and sought to keep people onside by acknowledging their domestic responsibilities.

> *How would a higher education and professional training act upon family life? Home duties fall to the lot of almost every woman, and nothing which tends to incapacitate for the performance of them ought to be encouraged.*[9]

Despite the positive arguments and the clear need for employment for women, many people held very negative opinions. It may seem amazing now, but as late as 1905 a senior physician wrote that domesticity was the natural sphere for women. He argued strongly that going into employment outside the home would reduce a woman's ability to have children, thus impacting negatively upon society and family life.

However, the world was changing. The Industrial Revolution had created new forms of employment, often at the expense of traditional ways of working. In 1857, Barbara Bodichon wrote *Women and Work,* a radical pamphlet in which she explored the arguments for women's education and employment to offer them financial independence. She paints a vivid picture of the changes that were driving the need for women's education.

> *Women in modern life, even in the humblest, are no longer spinsters. Their spinning is all done by the steam-engine; their sewing will soon be all done by that mighty worker. The work of our ancestresses is taken away from us; we must find fresh work. Idleness, or worse than idleness, is the state of tens of thousands of young women in Britain: in consequence, disease is rife amongst them; that one terrible disease, hysteria, in its multiform aspects, incapacitates thousands.*[10]

Ten years later, Elizabeth built upon these points. She was convinced that education would open up employment opportunities and thus reduce the number of girls who were abandoned to idleness. She argued that their energy and brain power could make them highly productive for the benefit of both themselves and society. But, despite these persuasive arguments, many men still regarded women as wholly responsible for domestic duties and believed that only men should be the breadwinners. To an extent, this view crossed class lines.

For middle-class women, there were two key questions: why did women seek employment, and could earning a wage be harmful? Even when families encouraged their daughters to have a broad education, they often opposed them going to work.

As a young girl, Florence Nightingale's (1820–1910) father encouraged her to learn and to read widely, but both her parents fought her desire to train as a nurse at Salisbury Infirmary; they believed that nursing was for the domestic servant class. Florence's mother was convinced that her daughter must have a hidden motive – probably an attachment to a disreputable surgeon!

Resistance was evident in the working class, too. In an 1840 publication, the Chartists argued strongly that it was undesirable for women to work, despite many working-class men needing their wives to supplement the family income. They still believed that domestic duties were for the women, while the men could work and enjoy leisure time. Even Mary Wollstonecraft acknowledged the dilemma of balancing work with motherhood, a dilemma still regularly explored in contemporary literature.

Over the years, social change played a key role in shifting opinions. The Poor Law Act of 1834 was based on the assumption that wives were dependents rather than significant contributors to family income. This view continued into the 1900s, despite evidence to the contrary. For example, work by William Booth in East London in the 1880s clearly showed that about 35% of families depended upon two incomes to survive.

As society changed, there were pragmatic reasons for women to be more active in the workplace. The Poor Law (1834) had made life very hard for a range of women in different circumstances, as highlighted by Beatrice Webb:

With regard to the really baffling problems, presented by the widow, the deserted wife of the absentee soldier or sailor, the wife of a husband resident in another parish or another country – with or without children – the Report is silent.[11]

The challenge of widowhood faced many women because typically they had a longer life expectancy. This was particularly evident among the working-classes, where men often died young because of workplace accidents and acute diseases. Women were more likely to suffer chronic diseases resulting from poor diet and multiple childbirth. By 1901, approximately 25% of married women aged forty-five to sixty-five were widowed.

It was feasible that a widow might move to seek work, but if she then had to apply for poor relief she could be sent back to the parish of her husband's birth, even if she had never been there before.

Deserted wives had no rights to poor relief and had to find a way to survive; for some, the only option was prostitution. Josephine Butler and Elizabeth were both convinced that education, industrial training and good employment could address these problems.

A strong influence on the debate about the employment of women came from single women. The 1851 census shows what was described as a 'surplus of women' in the population and yet, particularly in the middle classes, women were marginalised and could not undertake any financially rewarding work. Their very existence caused a public outcry and debate in many publications, from the *English Women's Journal* to *The Times*.

Large-scale emigration of working-class women started in the 1830s, and by the 1850s single middle-class women were also being encouraged to emigrate to the colonies. Ironically, it was made clear to them that they were emigrating to work and be independent, not to be idle or marry.

The numbers that went were fairly low, probably only two million between 1830 and 1900, of which only about 20% were single. However, with the involvement of feminists and the press, public opinion and middle-class culture shifted until women taking employment and remaining single became more acceptable.

The growth in the number of educated women took place alongside these shifts in opinion. As women gained an education, they could demand further training and their employment opportunities expanded. However, balancing work and motherhood was rarely possible; many educated women were required to resign when they married and fill their time with unpaid philanthropic projects, working for charities and voluntary organisations.

Employment: reality and opportunities

While middle-class women were still trapped in the domestic sphere, more working-class women were facing the harsh reality of mill life. During an 1844 House of Commons debate William Ferrand, a Yorkshire MP and passionate advocate for factory reform, offered a clear description of life for a female cotton-mill worker.

Half an hour to dress and suckle her infant and carry it out to nurse; one hour for household duties before leaving home; half an hour for actually travelling to the mill; twelve hours' actual labour; one and a half hours for meals; half an hour for returning home at night; one and half hours for household duties and preparing for bed, leaving six and half hours for recreation, seeing and visiting friends and sleep; and in winter, when it is dark half an hour extra time on the road to the mill and half an hour extra on road home from the mill.[12]

More than forty years later, Isabella Killick, an East London tailoress, presented a similar picture to the 1888 Parliamentary Committee. She was the main breadwinner because her husband was ill; she worked from six in the morning until eight at night to cover the rent and feed the family. Her own diet was severely inadequate, with meat twice a year if she was lucky. This overworked, underfed woman gave evidence to an audience of well-fed aristocratic men in a plush Westminster committee room; what a daunting experience it must have been and how brave she was.

The Factory Acts of the period were protective legislation that focused largely on the length of the working day. Many feminists supported working women in their fight against this legislation because it was an erosion of liberty and rights. Quite simply, for the poor working people fewer hours meant less pay and less food on the table.

Only as education became more accessible could women of all classes aim for better-paid employment. By late-Victorian times, approximately 4,000,000 girls and women were in paid employment in factory jobs, as domestic servants, shop assistants, clerical workers, agricultural labourers, small business owners, teachers, writers, actresses, and in hospitals. Women were literally on the move, travelling to work on trams and trains. The 1901 census shows that about 13% of married women were working for wages.

Action for employment

As employment and training became more available, women wanted employment that provided financial independence, self-respect and empowerment. Action was needed to break down prejudice and open up avenues for employment. Women needed practical and financial support, advice, role models and training. Elizabeth, and many other women, stepped up with action in the form of publications and associations.

Barbara Bodichon founded the Langham Place Group in 1857. This produced various journals that argued for employment and informed action, including the *English Woman's Journal* and Emily Faithfull's *Victoria Press*.

Langham Place was also the headquarters for the Society for Promoting the Employment of Women (SPEW), founded in 1859. This was an offshoot of the National Association for the Promotion of Social Science (NAPSS), of which Elizabeth was an active member. Jessie Boucherett established SPEW as an organisation run by women to bring about a revolution in female employment; its aims were to create a network of business contacts and promote opportunities. Boucherett's stated aims were to:

make it the business of her life to remedy or at least to
alleviate the evil by helping self-dependent women, not
with gifts of money, but with encouragement and training
for employments suited to their capabilities.[13]

SPEW adopted creative solutions that sometimes led to new opportunities for women-run businesses. For example, when a London company decided not to rebuild a china-painting studio after a fire, some of the women applied to SPEW for assistance. They gained funding to cover the period of rebuilding, getting new equipment and making new stock; the business went on to trade successfully once more, mainly with women employees. More than 170 years later, and with a new name (not surprisingly!), SPEW now exists as Futures for Women – but its principles are fundamentally the same.

The work of SPEW aligned closely with Elizabeth's views that the dire position of women resulted largely from their lack of skills. In 1866, she proposed a regional office and went on to establish one in Manchester. Elizabeth was following the example set by her colleague, Emily Davies, who had set up a similar office in Gateshead a few years earlier.

These women realised that it was vital to influence public opinion. They wrote regularly in the *English Woman's Journal* (EWJ). At the height of its popularity the EWJ had a monthly circulation of more than 1,000 copies, thus providing SPEW with a good base for challenging the belief that women were incapable of working outside the home and providing positive examples of women in both industrial trades and the professions.

In the *Victoria Press*, Emily Faithfull drew upon her

experiences in the USA to advocate for a wider range of employment opportunities for middle-class women. She acted as a role model for women working in printing; the *Victoria Press* was renowned for its position on women moving into male-dominated environments.

Economic demands and social changes gradually brought about a shift in opinion. The magazine *Queen*, which offered debates on the issues of the day, highlighted the question of employment for middle-class women and saw it as one of the most vexing questions at the time. Twenty years later, in the 1890s, this same magazine introduced a column of employment opportunities. This was a clear illustration of change.

In 1869, the Civil Service first employed women in the new telegraph service. The Postmaster General summarised numerous reasons for appointing them, including that they would not be eligible for long-service pay rises as they would retire upon getting married! In fact, they were paid seventy pence a week less than male colleagues; it was one hundred years later that the Dagenham strike in 1968 resulted in equal pay being enshrined in law – even if not always in practice. When the *Cassell's Family Magazine* wrote in 1876 about the Post Office Savings Bank appointing female clerks for the first time, the bank was inundated with applications and recruited seventy women.

Changing the face of education opened up opportunities for employment and this, in turn, empowered many women. Elizabeth worked tirelessly in both paid and voluntary roles to further the cause. She came to realise that a major barrier to freeing women was the constraints of marriage, so she went on to start a new campaign where her contribution made a radical difference to what many perceived as the slavery of women in marriage.

Chapter 4: Married life – heaven or hell?

Life as a Victorian wife

All marriages are different, yet they are the same in terms of the law of the time. Working-class and middle-class Victorian women had very different life experiences, but their marriages were subject to the same laws – laws that ignored them totally, making the women subservient and powerless.

Put bluntly, married women were invisible in the eyes of the law; a woman became an addition to what her husband owned, and he controlled everything. As Sir William Blackstone, an eighteenth-century judge and Tory politician, said:

> the husband and wife are one person in law; that is, the very being or legal existence of the woman is suspended during her marriage; or at least is incorporated or consolidated into that of her husband, under whose wing, protection and cover, she performs everything.[1]

In fact, the non-legal status kicked in once a woman accepted a proposal of marriage; she became a non-person. She could not dispose of property without her intended husband's consent; if she did sell anything during the engagement, she could be found guilty of fraud.

Yet society was changing slowly as more women actively pursued education and employment. Parallel with these changes, there was wider discussion and more written articles about the position of women. It was Elizabeth – and women like her – who adopted the cause and started pushing hard on many different fronts to change the law.

The feminists helped to change the legal position of married women in a number of aspects, thus enhancing their personal rights and boosting their self-respect. The areas that they addressed included divorce, ownership of property, childcare and domestic and sexual violence. That was quite an agenda and it required motivated, energetic and brave campaigners.

Elizabeth fought against the many injustices and inequalities married women experienced. This story, illustrating how mid-nineteenth-century law ignored the safety and rights of a wife and child, appeared in a pamphlet in the 1850s.

A drunken, violent husband was convicted of sexually abusing his ten-year-old daughter. The horrified wife wanted to protect the child and so moved to a distant part of the country. She changed her name and managed to support the two of them financially.

Imagine then her distress when the drunken husband tracked them down and turned up at her quiet cottage. Legally, he claimed her property, money and his rights to sexual activity.[2]

Divorce

Divorce was virtually impossible until the mid-1850s, even where a wife could prove she was suffering physical cruelty or financial deprivation.

The novel *Jane Eyre*, published in 1847 by Charlotte Bronte, illustrates how a wife, whatever her physical or mental condition, was completely in the power of the husband. In the novel, Mr Rochester has determined that his wife is mad, locked her up and taken control of all her property. Obviously, as readers we may not have a lot of sympathy for Mrs Rochester, who starts fires and bites people; she appears to be mentally unstable to the point of being dangerous. However, it is not a board of doctors or a court that rules on her condition and treatment; her husband decides simply to hide her away. Although the novel questions Mr Rochester's judgment in attempting a bigamous marriage with Jane, it doesn't seriously challenge his legal right to dispose of his existing wife as he chooses, much less her property.

This story may have been stimulated by a real case that started in the 1830s; certainly, it influenced some feminists. The fight to change the laws on divorce and access to children was started initially by a woman who was not a feminist but who experienced the horrors of an abusive relationship.

Caroline Sheridan Norton, the granddaughter of the playwright Richard Sheridan, took London society by storm in 1826, impressing all those she met with her beauty, wit and humour. She married George Norton, who turned out to be a cruel, abusive and jealous husband. In 1836, while she was visiting her brother, George sent their children away and refused Caroline any form of access to or contact with them. Distraught, she returned to her brother whilst her husband kept all her clothes, jewels and other possessions.

Norton let it be known in the press that she had left him and he would not pay any debts she incurred, leaving her penniless. Furthermore, he made unfounded allegations against her and accused her of adultery with the Prime Minister, Lord Melbourne.

Despite her desperate situation, Caroline's real focus was on her children. Through her efforts, an Infant Custody Bill was passed into law in 1839 which allowed mothers to apply to care for children under the age of seven; over that age, the mothers could apply for visits.

This case was much written about and discussed. It certainly influenced the young Barbara Bodichon and inspired her to take up the cause of women's rights. By 1857, she was the leader of the radical Langham Place Group (of which Elizabeth was a member), and she published many pamphlets explaining why women needed legal rights and financial independence.

Divorce was within the remit of the church until 1857, when the Divorce and Matrimonial Causes Act moved it into civil law. Feminists regarded the new law as very unsatisfactory because it maintained the double sexual standards prevalent in society: the husband could divorce the wife on grounds of adultery, while the wife needed a reason in addition to adultery, such as incest, rape, bigamy, cruelty or desertion. That double standard remained in law until 1923.

Divorce remained uncommon in the Victorian period for

various reasons, including the length of time the process demanded and fear of publicity. It was inconvenient and expensive, and fear of a disruption to the social order meant that divorced women were often ostracised.

However, the 1857 Act opened up the debate on the legal position of women and property ownership. Whereas a law changing divorce simply recognised the breakdown of a marriage, any legal changes to property ownership would recognise the existence of two individual people within an ongoing marriage. In the 1850s, most men could not envision a form of marriage where the husband and wife were equal in a political or economic sense.

The husband owns it all

Elizabeth worked tirelessly to achieve changes in the law relating to married women's rights to own property and keep the money they earned. The Victorian feminists challenged the law that kept women subservient and argued that the marriage and property laws violated a woman's right to freedom and equality. Unsurprisingly, they were often defeated by a Parliament whose male members wished to protect their own lifestyle and who saw family relationships as outside the jurisdiction of political justice.

In the mid-1800s, the husband really did own everything. The legal term 'coverture' (derived from the French verb to cover) captures the way in which the law regarded the wife as fully covered by her husband: it depersonalised the wife by means of a legal contract.

In society, property was a key mechanism for marking a person's position so women were placed at a severe disadvantage by not being able to own it. Gradually many women started to acknowledge this as outrageous and a form of state-sponsored robbery. Harriet Grove, a renowned thinker and the first love of the poet Shelley, who often referred to her husband as 'the Historian,' explained that she became a suffragist when:

> I discovered that the purse in my pocket and the watch at my side were not my own but the Historian's, I felt it was time women should have the power to amend these preposterous laws.[3]

Alongside the moves towards a divorce act in the 1850s, there was growing pressure to change the laws relating to property ownership. Barbara Bodichon and her colleagues wrote about this in various publications such as the *English Woman's Journal*; they wrote about the financial injustices and inequalities suffered by wives who, they argued, were in no better position financially than children.

In 1867, George Woodyatt Hastings[*] presented a paper at the Belfast Congress of NAPSS outlining the need for reform of the law relating to women's property. He recommended that English law should follow the example of New York State, which had recently given married women the same rights to property as unmarried women. In the autumn of that year, Elizabeth, Josephine Butler and Jessie Boucherett presented a proposal that they take the cause to the NAPSS executive committee. This was accepted, and so began the real fight to change the law.

---

[*] Hastings was secretary of the Law Amendment Society and Hon. Secretary of the National Reformatory Union. From 1857 to 1868 he was General Secretary of the National Association for Promotion of Social Science. In 1880 he became an MP.

Elizabeth already had a reputation as a woman who achieved results, so Jessie Boucherett visited her to persuade her to play a key role in the campaign. Despite still working full time, Elizabeth rose to the challenge; the Married Women's Property Committee was established in April 1868, with Elizabeth taking the important role of honorary secretary.

Once again, she was working alongside Josephine Butler. By December they had collected hundreds of signatures and started work on a draft bill; this was completed by February 1868 and introduced to Parliament two months later.

Their aim was to enshrine in law the right of a woman to keep the property she owned and any money she earned. Until the 1870 Act became law, no woman had a legal right to manage her finances. For some working-class women this meant that their husbands drank their wages rather than feeding their children; for some wealthy women, their land was sold to pay gambling debts. Legally, a husband had a responsibility to provide only basic subsistence level needs for his family. Only a new law could enable women to become financially independent and thus have greater control over how they chose to live and support their families.

Elizabeth's partner, Ben, shared her beliefs and supported her in practice. As the manager of a textile mill in Congleton, he paid the women's wages directly to them – something that the women appreciated but the men considered scandalous.

Building on the lessons she'd learned when working with Anti-Corn Law League and her campaigns for educational change, Elizabeth believed that it was vital to petition

Parliament to gain support for legal reforms. To this end, she wrote articles, gathered more than 100,000 signatures and issued more than 35,000 pamphlets, while also liaising with various regional groups.

The 1870 Act looked to be on track and was co-sponsored by John Stuart Mill until his defeat in the 1868 general election, but when the Bill went to the Lords in June 1870 it was greeted with a chorus of ridicule and disapproval. Its journey through the Commons had been similarly stormy; it was clear that men had very different opinions. Some supported giving women the vote but did not support this bill, perhaps because they wanted to preserve their own way of life and maintain domestic harmony. They believed it was the wife's responsibility to provide a peaceful and orderly home that offered their husbands a refuge from the public sphere.

Being the dominant male was perceived as a key element of masculinity, and some men were concerned that giving women economic freedoms would lead to arguments and diminish their personal power. Additionally, they saw these issues through the prism of social class; they believed that abuses of marriage were a problem of the working class and the state's intervention was only needed to protect what they defined as 'vulnerable' women.

The efforts of Elizabeth and many others finally achieved the passing of the 1870 Married Women's Property Act. Although it improved the position of wives to an extent, reformers soon identified problems. In late 1870, Elizabeth presented a paper to the NAPSS congress highlighting that the Act did not recognise the money that a woman had saved from her earnings *before* she married, or after she married but before the law had been passed, unless those earnings had been saved in a specific way set out in the Act.

Elizabeth wrote to *The Times* that the Act required a woman to take specific action to register savings or property; they did not automatically become hers by law. Another problem that she addressed was that the Act did not impose a responsibility on women for their debts. As Elizabeth pointed out in a paper submitted to NAPSS in 1875, this posed difficulties for married women running their own businesses. Suppliers were loath to supply goods on credit because money could not be legally recovered from them if they defaulted upon payment.

Despite the problems, the 1870 Act made the first change to the convention that a married woman was under the protection of her husband and had no legal existence. Based upon this partial success, some feminists felt that the problems with the Act could be left whilst they turned their attention to winning the vote for women.

In 1874, Elizabeth received a letter from Lydia E Baker that stated:

> *Dearest, – I am sorry about the decision respecting the M.W.P. ... I should be strongly averse to any attempt to re-open the question in the House of Commons until we have the vote* ... *let the whole matter lie over till the Suffrage Bill is passed.*[4]

Elizabeth, however, was not going to be detracted from her campaign; the work continued, and Dr Richard Pankhurst drafted a new Married Woman's Property bill. A respected radical Manchester attorney, he willingly drafted various bills that clearly identified the principle that married

---

* Underlining to denote italics in original text of the letter.

women should have the same rights as single women (the latter recognised in law as 'feme sole').

Richard Pankhurst was one of the original members of the council of NAPSS, which contributed to so many campaigns for women's emancipation. His radicalism and charismatic presentations attracted a young Emmeline Goulden; the attraction was mutual and they formed a powerful bond.

Sadly, on various occasions the MWP bill was passed without the change to enable married and single women to have the same rights, and the changes they strove for did not come into law until 1882. That was the year that Emmeline and Richard's daughter, Sylvia, was born – but they were possibly more thrilled by the Act being passed!

Writing later in her life, Sylvia notes that as the Bill progressed:

> Mrs Elmy strove the doubts and vacillations of legislators in the lobbies of Parliament. Ursula Bright, with her gracious charm, dined them and argued them into support.[5]

If this happened today, Elizabeth would probably be in the Westminster lobby ensuring she was interviewed by as many TV channels as possible while pressing any passing MPs to raise the issues at stake. The quote also highlights how these two women played to their personal strengths and social position.*

The Married Women's Property Act 1882 was judged to be fairer to all classes of society. It allowed a wife to both

---

* Ursula Bright, as the wife of an MP who supported the cause, had the opportunity and finances to wine and dine MPs while regaling them with her views.

keep and inherit money and property. She could: keep wages and investments she made and use them for herself, independently from her husband; inherit up to £200 in her own right and keep the money; keep any property inherited from her next of kin (if it was not bound in a trust) and inherit and hold rented property.

Finally, the law recognised women and allowed them to take control of their economic lives. Interestingly, although most of it has been repealed, Section 17 remains in force. This states that if there is a dispute between a husband and wife as to either's entitlement to, or share of, possessions or property, either party can apply to the Court for a judge to decide the share and make such Order as he thinks fit, including an Order for Sale.[*]

On 8 November 1882, the Married Women's Property Committee held its final meeting. Ursula Bright and Elizabeth were congratulated for their work and dedication to the cause. Elizabeth was noted specifically for her intellectual power, legal knowledge, practical skill and unflagging energy. This was reported in many national and regional newspapers.

Caring for children

Almost without stopping for breath, Elizabeth moved on to the legal injustice faced by married women in relation to childcare and access.

Her efforts to improve the rights of women were frequently considered from the perspective of children and

---

[*] https://www.ringroselaw.co.uk/2016/08/02/18055/ Sourced 09/02/2021.

their needs. During a lifetime of campaigning, she raised the issues of childbirth, custody of infants and infant mortality. She spoke and wrote widely on these topics and sought to ensure that laws were fair and equal.

In 1880 Elizabeth delivered a speech in London entitled 'The criminal code in its relation to women'. One quote from this illustrates how the law placed unrealistic expectations on pregnant women of all classes. Here she quotes Section 181 of the Criminal Code:

> Every woman is guilty of a crime who, being with child, and being about to be delivered, neglects to provide reasonable assistance in her delivery, if the child is permanently injured ... or dies either just before or during or just after birth, unless she proves that such a death was not caused by such neglect... [6]

Set within the context of desperate poverty, high mortality rates and a lack of modern maternity services, this has the potential to make a criminal of any pregnant woman. This law not only criminalised abortion but targeted women who could not seek effective support during childbirth, even though they might not be able to afford such support or it was simply not available.

As discussed, the Norton case resulted in the passing of the Custody of Infants Act in 1839 making a mother responsible for the welfare of the child until it was seven years old, after which the state recognised only the father as its guardian. When a wife left a violent husband, she had no right to keep her children. If the husband chose to evict his wife after a false accusation of adultery, he kept the children. Even the death of a much-loved husband could result in the children being removed from their mother.

Elizabeth argued for the rights of the child and for co-equal rights of both parents. She spoke at the NAPSS* national conference in 1877 and wrote persuasively about the importance of both parents in raising children, saying that nature herself intended this by giving a child two parents. This discussion surely continues in many homes today.

Her work and radical views strongly influenced the Guardianship of Infants Act 1886. This took two-and-a-half years to go through Parliament and was significantly changed during its passage despite Elizabeth's efforts, yet it made some major changes. The Act gave women more chance of achieving custody of their children after being divorced and stipulated that the welfare of the child should be taken into consideration, thereby undermining the father's automatic right to custody. It also recognised a widow's right to have custody of her children after the death of her husband.

In addition to her articles and speeches, Elizabeth produced 280 petitions containing over 28,000 signatures in respect of this bill. One can certainly agree with the statement of one of her colleagues: 'How this woman works!'

We have all heard worries about standards of childcare and how to pay for it while the mother goes to work. These concerns are still very pertinent today, and they were ones that Elizabeth and her colleagues recognised. In her writing, she demonstrated an understanding that working women had few choices: to leave children unattended for hours, or

---

* NAPSS – National Association for the Promotion of Social Science.

in the care of a family friend, or to pay for someone, which would reduce the money available for food and rent.

Elizabeth and other feminists were outraged by the phrase 'baby farming' that was popularised in the 1860s following two cases that scandalised the public. This derogatory term described any situation where a woman accepted money in exchange for caring for a child that was not her own, particularly illegitimate children and the children of widows who had to pay for care while they worked. The service was often provided by those who could not do other work due to age or disability, and it provided them with some income. The cases led to the Infant Life Protection Act 1872, and, like other laws, it enshrined a double standard: it allowed for the policing of women's child-rearing practices rather than forcing the father to share financial responsibility for his children.

Elizabeth was also concerned for the mothers of children born outside marriage. The Poor Law of 1834 made the mother, whatever her circumstances, wholly responsible for their care. The Bastardy Law Amendment Act in 1872 was carelessly drafted and left women with no legal redress for a child born before the passing of the Act.

In September 1872, the *Women's Suffrage Journal* reported on two ways in which the Act failed to serve women and their illegitimate children. On 22 August, a Manchester magistrate heard a case against a man proven to be the father of an illegitimate baby. The mother was granted support, only to be called back as she left the court. The magistrate realised that the baby had been born before the Bill (passed into law on 10 August), so the father left the court with no further financial commitments for the child.

The article reported that the Act had included a limit of five shillings* a week that a man could be asked to pay. This meant that a wealthy man who might, for example, have got a young servant girl pregnant, would only contribute enough for very basic care. Elizabeth fought to have the Act amended and, in the meantime, helped women trapped by the defective law.

It was clear that caring for children and economic independence were interrelated. Although many people wished to divide issues along class lines, class simply meant that women experienced the issues differently. This also applied to domestic violence, which many sought to identify solely as a working-class matter although this was definitely not the case.

Domestic and sexual violence

A spaniel, a woman and a walnut tree, the more they're beaten the better they be.
Old English Proverb.[7]

Although Elizabeth was involved in challenging domestic and sexual violence from the early 1880s, she wrote to her friend Harriet McIlquhan in 1897 that:

It is the fear of men that women will cease to be any longer their sexual slaves either in or out of marriage that is the root of the whole opposition to our just claim [women's suffrage]. No doubt their fear is justified, for that is precisely what we do mean.[8]

Elizabeth will no doubt have seen Punch and Judy shows

---

* The previous Act had set the limit at two shillings and six pence.

many times as they were popular street entertainments during her lifetime. Some saw them as essentially harmless, even funny, while others criticised the performances for glorifying domestic violence.

One doubts that Elizabeth saw humour in the shows because she recognised that many women experienced domestic and sexual violence at the hands of their husbands. She first raised the issue of domestic violence as early as 1874 in papers she presented at conferences. Sadly, however, domestic violence still blights the lives of both women and men today.

The Punch and Judy shows certainly contrasted with the image of the Victorian middle class as genteel and morally upright, yet much was written in the mid-Victorian period about husband and wife as master and slave. Although there was a desire to make domestic violence a class issue, the truth is that it was easier to hide violence in a large, middle-class family where the emphasis was on privacy and preserving the image of the ideal home. For working-class people in cramped, shared accommodation, violence was more visible. Emotional abuse was not recognised at the time, but there is no doubt that women of all classes suffered when their husbands diminished their wives' self-esteem and exerted control over their lives.

The Clitheroe case in 1891 highlighted the behaviour of some men and illustrated the views being publicised in the press. Emily and Edmund Jackson married in 1887; he then left her and went to live abroad for three years. Upon his return, she refused to see him. As she left church in Clitheroe one Sunday, Edmund and some of his associates abducted her and locked her up in a house. He claimed in court that a husband was entitled to keep his wife in confinement to enforce his conjugal rights. The Court of Appeal heard in her favour, but some newspaper reports showed sympathy for the husband; *The Times* declared the Court of Appeal decision as the abolition of marriage in England.

Writers of the period such as Frances Power Cobbe, a social reformer and suffrage campaigner, recognised domestic violence in all classes; others argued that violence occurred when wives failed to be deferential and did not act suitably to pacify their husbands. So, let's blame the women and then batter them! Men rarely blamed themselves but justified their behaviour as necessary to enforce order in the home.

Some writers reinforced the view that domestic violence only happened among the working class. Temperance groups focused on the ills of drink, while others felt a husband might resort to violence in response to 'nagging, taunts and insults and any form of wilful behaviour on the wife's part', thus causing the husband to 'show her who the boss is around here'. The law was definitely on the husband's side; even when a case went to court, the judge would focus upon keeping the couple together regardless of the evidence.

A series of five 'Ripper' murders in August 1888 raised public awareness of violence towards women. However, campaigns against marital violence pre-dated these murders by at least ten years.

Frances Power Cobbe wrote an influential article in

1878 in the *Contemporary Review Journal**, which included details of how economic dependency made it difficult for women to leave an abusive marriage. She wrote graphically about women being hesitant to report their husbands for fear of reprisal, and told the grisly tale of a woman who appeared in court without a nose and claimed she had bitten it off herself. This illustrates how some women lived in fear and were manipulated both physically and emotionally by their husbands.

Feminists of the period believed that violence was rooted in lack of equality. In 1874, Elizabeth started a campaign against domestic violence that was important in gaining support for the Matrimonial Causes Act of 1878. This enabled victims of domestic violence to obtain a protection order from a magistrates' court. As this was not a divorce, it was much less costly and therefore available to all women, including those in the working class.

Sadly, we still need similar campaigns today. Statistics in this field can be unreliable, but it is on record that the police forces across England and Wales receive a call about domestic abuse EVERY HOUR of EVERY DAY,** which does not include violence to women outside the home.

---

* The journal was established in 1866 as a forum for open inquiry into theological and philosophical issues of the day.

** Source: https://www.womensaid.org.uk/information-support/what-is-domestic-abuse/how-common-is-domestic-abuse/ Accessed 27/02/2021.

Marital rape

The husband cannot be guilty of a rape committed by himself upon his lawful wife, for by their mutual consent and contract the wife hath given up herself in this kind unto her husband, which she cannot retract.[9]

A man does not commit rape by having sexual intercourse with his lawful wife, even if he does so by force and against her will.[10]

These quotes were written more than two hundred years apart, one in England and the other in the USA but, despite this, they express the same view. The first was written by Sir Matthew Hale in England and published posthumously in 1736; the second, about US law, was by Rollin Perkin in 1957.

In the Victorian era marital rape was not a topic for discussion, despite many women wanting to avoid conceiving more children to protect their own health and avoid placing a greater financial burden on a large family. One imagines most women simply accepted the situation and believed it was their duty. With the deafening silence surrounding the topic, only a courageous woman would stand up and name it on a public platform. Step forward Elizabeth.

In March 1880, she addressed a London meeting of the Dialectical Society* with a speech entitled 'The criminal

---

* This society was founded in London in 1867 for professionals. A group was later established in Boston, USA; Martin Luther King Jr. addressed it in 1954.

code in relation to women'. She spoke about Hale's view on rape and how this was enshrined in the Criminal Code; this defined rape as the act of a man, over the age of fourteen years, having carnal knowledge of a woman who was not his wife without her consent. In other words, a husband could not be guilty of raping his wife. Elizabeth stated clearly that she perceived this as state-condoned domestic violence.

This was strong stuff: marital rape had been given a name. Even so, it was only the start of a very long road. In England and Wales, the first statutory definition of rape was within the Sexual Offences (Amendment) Act in 1976. Marital rape in England and Wales was not recognised until 1991, more than one hundred years after it was named by Elizabeth in public. In October 1991, the Law Lords unanimously swept away the old laws that made marital rape legal.

Sexual violence against women and girls still happens, often as a weapon of war, but the importance of women's sexual rights and self-determination is being recognised increasingly as crucial to women's rights.

In 2012, Navi Pillay, the High Commissioner for Human Rights, presented information to show that violations of women's human rights were often linked to their sexuality and reproductive role. She explained how married women in many countries cannot refuse sexual relations with their husbands, and yet such rights are fundamental to a life of dignity.

Sexual and reproductive rights are human rights. They are not new rights, and they are not optional. They are intrinsic to a range of internationally binding treaties. At the very core of these rights is the autonomy of every human being, which involves deeply personal issues such as whether, when, how and with whom any individual chooses to have sex; whether, when, and whom one chooses to marry; whether, when, how and with whom one chooses to have children; and how we choose to express gender and sexuality.[11]

Can you hear Elizabeth cheering this speech? But one imagines she would be horrified at such slow progress and be campaigning vigorously for women everywhere.

Marriage for a Victorian woman could be heaven or hell, and they had no legal support to call upon. The range of Elizabeth's work demonstrates her ability to appreciate how social and economic issues are interrelated – and that there are no simple answers.

Her writing, speaking and campaigning informed and engaged those in power, and she succeeded in changing the legal and economic position for many women. The passing of the Married Women's Property Acts was highly significant in raising the awareness and understanding of those in power for the need for change. Some felt this should have been set aside to focus upon gaining the vote; Elizabeth's judgement was sound, however, and she played a vital role in bringing into law one of the main legal changes of the nineteenth century. Marriage for some remains a state of control and fear, but Elizabeth's efforts shifted the majority view and positively influenced the lives that many of us lead today.

As we move into the next area of her work, it is clear that Elizabeth was not only concerned about the sexual violation of married women but also the fate of unmarried women and young girls.

Chapter 5: No sex please ...
without equality

Elizabeth was concerned about inequality in laws relating to prostitution and the lack of sexual education for young women. The Victorians tended to regard sexual ignorance as a feminine virtue, yet this left young women prey to sexual violence and to having large families, leading to economic and physical hardship and emotional pain.

Elizabeth was involved with reforms to the Contagious Diseases Acts and campaigning for sex education. Both were radical concepts that demanded action from women of courage and strong principles.

Contagious Diseases Acts (CDAs)

What campaign could unite Florence Nightingale, male doctors, some first-wave feminists and working men? The answer is the fight against the Contagious Diseases Acts (CDAs).

Elizabeth will have witnessed – and possibly known – hardworking women who were forced to choose between prostitution and the horrors of the workhouse. This may well have encouraged her to protest against laws that she saw as the state-sponsored abuse of the female body.

Her colleague, Josephine Butler, regarded these laws as instrumental rape by the state. Between 1864 and 1886, the law allowed the police to intimidate and inflict intimate physical abuse on women. Sadly, this resulted in numerous suicides.

Elizabeth viewed the CDAs as *sexual legislation of the basest kind [and] class legislation of the cruellest kind.*[1]

A Royal Commission in 1857 on the health of the Army had identified the prevalence of sexually transmitted diseases. The first Act was passed in 1864 to control these diseases among enlisted men and reflected a new interventionist approach to social problems.

This problem had previously been identified in garrison towns and ports overseas. The basis of the CDAs was initially implemented in the British colonies of India and Hong Kong. Initially the authorities proposed inspecting the men but this was considered demeaning; that did not concern them when it came to women.

In 1864 the Director General of the Medical Department wrote in *The Lancet* that:

> the only sure means of mitigating the ravages of syphilis, and probably in causing its entire disappearance, is to superintend, by compulsory examination and cure, the health of the public women who propagate it.[2]

This article resulted in a bill being taken to Parliament, though there was debate about what to call it. 'Contagious Diseases' was a phrase usually associated with legislation related to animals, so there was some initial confusion, but it was feared that a more accurate name might cause distress to the MPs' wives and daughters. They considered putting 'women' or 'not animals' in brackets as part of the

Bill title, but finally decided on simply using 'Contagious Diseases'.

Building on the 1864 Act, the CDAs passed in 1866 and 1869 were informed by social attitudes and views about women, sexuality and class. These two acts extended the application to all areas of the country, in addition to extending their powers. The 1864 Act required prostitutes to undergo an internal inspection by a doctor, as described by John Stuart Mill.

Typically, the woman's legs were clamped open and her ankles tied down. Surgical instruments – sometimes not cleaned from a prior inspection – were inserted so inexpertly that some women miscarried. Others passed out from the pain or embarrassment.[3]

If a woman refused to be examined, she could be held until she submitted; even if she were proved innocent of prostitution, clearing her name would be prohibitively costly. If she continued to refuse an examination, she could be sent to prison (which might include hard labour). If a girl was discovered to be a virgin, she was given five shillings and told to have a hot meal.

The 1866 Act allowed for plain-clothed police to patrol areas and require suspected prostitutes to undergo fortnightly internal inspections for up to one year. The 1869 Act required prostitutes to carry an official registration card.

Despite a law that made prostitutes into criminals, prostitution was recognised as fulfilling an important service for men's innate sexual desires – desires that no genteel wife could surely be expected to fulfil!

The Royal Commission set up in 1871 to investigate

the implementation of the Acts clearly shows the double standard by stating that:

...we may at once dispose of any recommendation founded on the principle of putting both parties to the sin of fornication on the same footing by the obvious but not less conclusive reply that there is no comparison to be made between the prostitutes and the men who consort with them. With the one sex the offence is committed as a matter of gain; with the other it is an irregular indulgence of a natural impulse.[4]

The hypocrisy is clear: male sexuality required prostitutes, but females offering this service could be held as criminals and subjected to highly intrusive medical examinations against their wishes. It was also likely that some women who were not prostitutes were accused and subjected to these laws.

Opposition to these acts started in 1869, although the first campaigners were regarded as eccentric cranks. The National Association for the Repeal of the Contagious Diseases Acts was established to lobby Parliament and, although it initially excluded women, Elizabeth attended one of its meetings in early December 1869. She was outraged and determined to fight these degrading laws, and it became one of the most important campaigns of her life.

She was so outraged about the Acts, and no doubt about the exclusion of women from the national association, that she contacted Josephine Butler. They moved quickly and by late December 1869 had formed the Ladies National Association (LNA), which became very influential in the campaign for repeal.

Contacting Josephine was an inspired act because she

was a charismatic leader and speaker, and many people regarded her as highly moral which was an advantage when discussing such a delicate subject. By the end of 1869, the LNA had collected more than one hundred signatures and published an article in a daily newspaper outlining how the Acts violated women's legal safety and gave the police undue powers over them.

The LNA went on to establish nearly sixty regional offices. The press was both astonished and perplexed by women's involvement in such a distasteful subject. The *Spectator Saturday Review* described them as 'the shrieking sisterhood'. However, by the mid-1870s the LNA had gained support from many nonconformist church groups and sponsorship from the Liverpool Working Men's National League.

Despite still working as a headmistress and being involved in other campaigns, Elizabeth spoke and wrote widely against these laws. At a NAPSS[*] conference in Bristol, she highlighted their inherent double standards. In her private correspondence she referred to the 'male sex bias' that was based on the belief that male sexual desire was a need like breathing that must be satisfied. Women's bodies could be regulated by law to ensure men fulfilled their physical needs.

In her public writing, Elizabeth stressed the dangers of criminalising women who were not prostitutes but who happened to live near places where prostitutes worked or converged. In a pamphlet for the LNA, she wrote:

The law is ostensibly framed for a certain class of women,

---

[*] NAPSS – National Association for the Promotion of Social Science.

but in order to reach these, all women residing within the district where it is in force are brought under the revisions of the Acts. Any woman can be dragged into court, and required to prove that she is not a common prostitute. The magistrate can condemn her, if a policeman swears only that he 'has good cause to believe' her to be one. The accused has to rebut, not positive evidence, but the state of mind of the accuser.[5]

The LNA's action didn't stop at writing and speaking at meetings. During an electoral campaign in 1870 to challenge MPs supporting the laws, women were chased from Colchester by brothel keepers and other bullies. Another time they faced mortal danger when a hay loft where they were holding an anti-CDA meeting was set alight. Many of the campaigners were threatened with sexual violence – an early indication of what suffragettes would face many years later.

Elizabeth demonstrated her innate courage throughout the campaign. Although many supporters of women's rights deplored the CDAs, only a small number of them actively supported the campaign because they were fearful of tarnishing their reputation.

She was also innovative in communicating her message and started doing mailshots, for which she became renowned.

The campaign gained support from a broad range of people, including the National Medical Association, the nonconformist churches, and working men. The latter sent a delegation to the Home Secretary in 1872 stating that:

A resolution of the Workingmen's National League is evidence of their views: This meeting considers that the

Contagious Diseases Acts relating to women are a cruel
and shameful evil and an injustice to working women . . .
by placing their reputations and their persons at the mercy
of an irresponsible secret police, they are a violation of
the principles of our laws which require the accuser to
prove his charge before the accused is called upon to
prove her innocence ... Nothing short of their immediate
and total repeal will suffice to allay the widespread and
increasing indignation with which they are regarded by
the working classes.[6]

Activity increased during the 1870s. At a public meeting
in March 1870, John Stuart Mill stated that the Acts resulted in the wives and daughters of the poor being exposed
to insufferable indignities based upon the suspicion of
a policeman. The following year both he and Josephine
Butler appeared before the 1871 Royal Commission into the
administration of the Acts. Stuart Mill spoke vociferously
against them because they opposed the fundamental
principle of personal liberty. Josephine Butler spoke equally
passionately, and it is recorded that many in the audience
responded positively to her magnetic appeal.

Nevertheless, there was strong opposition. William
Acton, whose paper to the Association of Medical Officers
of Health was instrumental in the extension of the CDAs
to the civilian population, said that he was hostile to
prostitutes and also to those who opposed the Acts; such
women challenged the male-dominated medical profession
and publicly discussed an unsavoury subject that was
inappropriate for the fair sex.

We can assume that Elizabeth played a significant role
in gaining support and collecting signatures for the many

petitions against CDAs. In 1882, the Select Committee on Petitions of the House of Commons reported that the number presented to the House since 1870 concerning the CDAs totalled 10,315; these had a staggering 2,015,404 signatures. These figures would be impressive today, with TV, radio, social media and twenty-four-hour news spreading the word, but Victorian campaigners had to rely on word of mouth, meetings and the printed word. By comparison, only forty-five petitions (3,579 signatures) were submitted in support of the Acts.

The hard work eventually paid off and the Acts were repealed in 1886. There had been seventeen years of hard campaigning, seventeen years when women suffered invasive treatment to allow men to degrade prostitutes and those suspected of being prostitutes.

As early as 1870, the impact of this outcome was recognised by Daniel Cooper[*] when he addressed the LNA:

At this crisis we heard that the women of England were waking up to the consideration of this question. We were rejoiced beyond measure when we saw the announcement of your Ladies' Association in opposition to the Acts... We felt on hearing of your Association that Providence had well chosen the means for the defeat of these wicked Acts. The ladies of England have saved the country from this fearful curse; for I fully believe that through them it has had its death blow. But for the Ladies Association we should have had no discussion, and the Acts would have by this date have probably been extended throughout the country.[7]

---

[*] Daniel Cooper had formed the Society for Rescue of Young Women and Children in 1853.

Sexual ignorance or education

Women were expected to be ignorant about sex; this no doubt led to many unwanted pregnancies and may also account for the assumption that women had no sexual desire or passion. Many people regarded sex education as no better than pornography; the purpose of marriage was to produce children, even though large families might impact negatively on the family's finances and the wife's health.

Since it was considered a virtue for females to be ignorant about their bodies, girls probably had little understanding of menstruation or how they might become pregnant. These issues concerned Elizabeth and her partner, Ben.

The idea that a woman might actually enjoy sex was not addressed by a wide audience until the middle of the twentieth century and, even then, it was literature that often led the way. D.H. Lawrence and Hemingway (writing how 'the earth moved') were both influential authors.

Between 1860 and the 1880s, the size of middle-class families declined, in part because of more information becoming available about birth control. Elizabeth played her part by providing sex education for young people and writing about free love, which she and Ben practised before having to get married.*

Elizabeth and Ben, writing under the pseudonym of Ellis Ethelmer, wrote three books on this topic. Although simple in style, they were influential; Marie Stopes certainly built on them in her own work. The idea of sex education was radical then, as it still is in many parts of the world today.

---

* Marriage was forced upon them due to Elizabeth becoming pregnant. This is discussed in Chapter 8.

The Human Flower, published in 1894, was intended for older children. The front cover states that it is about the physiology of birth and relations between the sexes, and it is clearly intended to answer the questions children often ask: 'how did I come into existence?' and 'where did I come from?'. The book uses imagery from the animal and plant worlds to offer simple, inoffensive answers.

The Human Flower took a broad perspective on sexual activity. In Chapter 6 it warns against premarital sex, not for fear of losing one's virginity or virtue but because an unmarried mother had no legal status and a child born out of wedlock would experience harsh treatment and probably grow up in a workhouse. The book also addressed the fact that a Victorian wife had to bear her husband as many children as he 'chose to impose on her'.

Elizabeth and Ben's fundamental belief in equality is obvious. They suggested that men shared the responsibility for parenting and concluded by stating that humanity would be advanced by the reciprocal union of male and female intelligences and qualities, rather than the forced control of one by the other.

Are the male flowers of a vegetable marrow plant need-less, or do they lead a useless life; seeing that they bear no fruit?[8]

Reading this now, it appears a simple, innocuous question about plants but it is a quote from *Baby Buds*, which Elizabeth and Ben published in 1895. They were talking about sex.

In *Woman Free* (1893), they used verse to explore the nature of relationships and how they could be positive for both partners. Thus, the verse moves from 'carnal servitude' and 'sexual wrong' to:

Thus learn we that in woman rendered free
Is raised the rank of humanity;[9]

The books were written from the belief that knowledge of sexuality and sexual health could help to prevent violence and trauma in adult relationships. Elizabeth and Ben wanted to eradicate the ignorance and misinformation that was often shared through whispers and embarrassed conversations. They stated that ignorance makes all sexual activity an act of coercion; no true love can exist where sexual desire by one partner is forced upon a reluctant partner.

In writing these books, their aims were to stimulate open, honest education of young people in sexual matters and encourage constancy and respect in love; they were also keen to enable women to control pregnancy.

♦ ♦ ♦

These issues illustrate the breadth of Elizabeth's work, her energy and her bravery. By openly tackling such radical topics as sex education, she (and Ben) laid a strong foundation upon which many have built since. One could argue that their views on equality are still being pursued today.

The fight against the CDAs took years. It demanded late nights, hard work and resilience in the face of criticism. Elizabeth demonstrated how, even without the vote, women were becoming adept at taking on a strong political role. It was during this fight that she extended her influential work and truly became the Parliamentary watchdog with a bite.

Chapter 6: The watchdog with a bite

Women had no right to vote and no opportunity to become an MP. Although the Victorian period was an era of great change on many fronts, the greatest resistance to change was the legal position of women – yet they did wield power and influence. How?

Elizabeth (and others) understood the power of the pen and wrote articles for journals and newspapers in addition to pamphlets. Despite some of them hesitating to be the focus of attention in a mixed audience, others, like Josephine Butler, were charismatic public speakers. During the CDA campaigns, these women gained notoriety for speaking about the sensitive topics of sexuality and prostitution.

Elizabeth used her understanding of how to exert power from outside the formal political arena to place pressure on Parliament. Through petitions and letters to MPs, she gained a reputation as a watchdog with a bite. This was confirmed by the key roles she played within two organisations, the Personal Rights Association, and the Women's Emancipation Union. Both were influential and held to their purpose of changing the position of women in society.

Personal Rights Association (PRA)

In 1871, Elizabeth and Josephine Butler formed an organisation that took a broad perspective and influenced numerous laws. From their experiences in challenging the CDAs[*] they were aware of tensions among middle-class radicals, some of whom wished to focus solely on gaining the vote. There was also a growing divide between the political interests of working-class men and women.

Elizabeth and Josephine formed the Committee for Amending the Law in Points Injurious to Women (CALPIW), with an initial focus on laws relating to the protection of infant life. The following year it went through a name change and became the Personal Rights Association (PRA); the first title may have said what it did, but it didn't trip off the tongue. The PRA continued its work until 1978, showing once again how Elizabeth's work has had a lasting impact on British society.

Her involvement with the PRA demonstrates her determination to take on a broad range of activities; she was resistant to dedicating her efforts to single goal of gaining the vote. She had to leave teaching in 1871 because of her secularism, and this gave her the opportunity to become secretary within the PRA. Once again, she was a trail blazer as she was the first woman to have such a paid role.

The PRA was on a quest to achieve equality in all aspects of social, political, economic and sexual aspects of life. This fitted well with Elizabeth's wish to address a range of topics because the PRA was diverse in its interests; amongst other issues, it dealt with laws against women's labour, equality

---

[*] CDAs – Contagious Diseases Acts.

of parenthood and compulsory medical examinations of women, for example in cases of infanticide.

The stated purpose was to achieve equality in all aspects of the law. A PRA pamphlet[1] stated the purpose and aims as:

OBJECT OF THE ASSOCIATION.

The object of the Association is to uphold the principle of the perfect equality of all persons before the law in the exercise and enjoyment of their Individual Liberty within the widest practicable limits.

It seeks the attainment of this object—

- *I.—By labouring to effect the repeal of all existing laws which directly or indirectly violate the aforesaid principle.*
- *II.—By opposing the enactment of all new laws which violate the said principle.*
- *III.—By promoting such amendments of the law and its administration as are necessary for giving practical effect to that principle.*
- *IV.—By watching over the execution of the laws so as to guard the maintenance of that principle, in so far as it has already received legislative sanction, and to show the evil results of its violation when laws or administrative methods are carried out in disregard of it.*
- *V.—By spreading among the people a knowledge of the rights and liberties to which they are or ought to be legally entitled, and of the moral grounds on which those legal rights and liberties are founded.*

The PRA developed views that represented a shift from

a feminist base to one that had a more humanitarian perspective based upon equality. Their aims illustrate how they focused upon challenging sexual and political domination in a way that pursued egalitarian justice in society, politics and economics. Their work also provides a clear illustration of male domination at the time, and how laws continued to maintain female subjection.

The principle quoted above highlights the aim of working for perfect equality of all people, so they collaborated with men of power who shared their views. In 1877, Peter A. Taylor, Liberal MP for Leicester, addressed the PRA and spoke eloquently about how women, by being denied rights of citizenship, were denied opportunities for doing good and consequently were a loss to society.

Being open to working with men enabled the PRA to engage with some of the most radical thinkers and politicians, many of whom had campaigned against the Corn Laws and supported women's suffrage. The press could be very unkind to such men, describing them in derogatory terms usually applied to women, such as 'fussy' and 'busybodies'.

Despite its small membership, the PRA was able to make a great noise and raise awareness through its many channels of publicity. It is fair to say that it had a larger influence on politics than its size would suggest due to the tenacious approach of women such as Elizabeth, who used all available options to build support and maintain pressure on politicians. In addition to the national press, the PRA had its own journal, first published in 1881.

By being a founder member and taking on a key role in the PRA, Elizabeth's life was immediately different in every sense. She left behind the structure of teaching and moved to a more flexible lifestyle, with an annual salary of £300 (equivalent to approximately £40,000 today). Moving from the north, she was based in London where she spent her time writing, in meetings and planning events. She travelled the country frequently to address groups on a wide range of topics. She published widely in journals and magazines, and her writing illustrates how she saw the interlinking themes of poverty, social tension and sexual voraciousness as being catalysts for human despair.

Through her writing and speaking, she gained a positive reputation. She was recognised as being acerbic, forthright and challenging or, to put that another way, she said it as she saw it. Among those who recognised her work was the editor of the *Northern Echo*, who regarded her as the soul of the PRA.

Elizabeth engaged with numerous campaigns; in doing so, she showed some of the MPs that not only was she acting as a watchdog, she had a bite!

Infant Life Protection Act (1872). As previously discussed, in the 1860s the phrase 'baby farming' entered the English language. This derogatory term was used to both condemn and marginalise child carers, many of whom were needed by working women, although clearly there were cases where these women acted without any proper care for the babies. The following letter was published in *The British Medical Journal*:[2]

> *A physician writes to us in the following strain. "Several years ago, I held the appointment of medical officer at the Sick Children's Hospital in Manchester, where many sad instances of the effects of baby-farming came under*

my notice ... Numerous were the cases of diarrhoea and atrophy from mesenteric disease ... The majority were brought when the child was so near death the nurse believed a death certificate would be wanted. The diseases which the farmed children suffered could be traced in nearly all cases to improper food and, in some cases, to insufficient food.

The Act introduced the legal right to monitor women's child-rearing practices, rather than place any attention on forcing fathers to pay for the upkeep of their offspring. It represented a creeping encroachment of the state on the home and, like others Acts passed around this time, it reinforced the notion that a woman's natural duties were to nurture children and care for men while the men worked and had political power.

The PRA was keen to show how the legal spotlight was wrongly aimed at women, and that withdrawing childcare would significantly reduce the chances women supporting themselves. It did not hold back from showing how the law placed responsibility on women; similar arguments have been made in recent times about child support.

Elizabeth, Josephine Butler and other PRA members wrote a powerful pamphlet entitled *Infant Mortality: its causes and remedies.* As well as arguing that the law would restrict women's ability to work and support a family, it highlighted that infant mortality was frequently due to ignorance and poverty, the seduction of young women causing unwanted pregnancies, and the difficulty unmarried mothers had in finding employment to provide for themselves and their children, rather than the actions of child carers. The PRA appreciated that eradicating poverty would take years (though one doubts they expected it to remain with us well over one hundred years later) and, in the short term, argued for laws that raised the age of consent to reduce the seduction of young girls.

Factory Act (1874). Writing about factory conditions before this Act, the historian Edward P. Thompson describes the exploitation of young children as one of the most shameful events in British history. The 1874 Act built upon previous legislation; amongst other things it, raised the minimum working age to nine and limited the working day for women and young children to ten hours in the textile industry. Other Acts applied similar restrictions in other industries.

One would think that Elizabeth and her colleagues would fully support such an Act but, although she probably applauded the Bill's intentions with regard to children, Elizabeth recognised its serious implications for working women. She encouraged the PRA to challenge the Bill because it was another example of how the law was making it harder for women to earn enough money to avoid poverty and destitution. It placed women in a box as domestic and reproductive creatures and took away their freedom to decide how they lived and worked.

The various Acts were confusing and difficult to monitor by the factory inspectors, so a Royal Commission was set up in 1875 to consider how the laws could be consolidated. The Commission heard evidence from women who strongly opposed having their hours restricted by law. This encouraged Elizabeth and her colleagues to write another pamphlet, *Legislative Restrictions on the Industry of Women, considered from the women's point of view.* By including the voices of working women from Leeds and

Nottingham, they provided examples of how the proposed law could oppress working women and make it hard for them to earn much-needed money.

In 1874, Elizabeth asked the Trades Union Congress to invite a group of women and listen to their concerns. When this request was rejected, she realised that the men were not interested because it did not directly affect them and their own working hours. She raised this with her colleagues and the MP Jacob Bright, an important figure in these circles. The matter was discussed at the NAPSS conference in Bristol, and this led to the creation of the National Union of Women Workers.

The PRA's work on factory legislation crossed numerous boundaries and brought changes in how working women could seek to influence legislation that would impact upon their work and economic standing.

Section 40 Marine Mutiny Bill. This attracted the attention of Elizabeth and the PRA for its potential impact on women. Section 40 stated that no member of the serving forces could be compelled to support financially any of his relations who were destitute. Many of the wives and children of these men depended upon them for financial support. The PRA was quick to draw the attention of those who would be faced with destitute families to this, namely local government officials and Boards of Guardians. Subsequently changes were made to the Bill; the PRA's action increased awareness of how public attention could be attracted to such issues.

Contagious Diseases Acts. In the previous chapter, we saw how Elizabeth and Josephine Butler campaigned vigorously against the CDAs and finally succeeded in having them repealed in 1886.

As part of her campaign, Elizabeth encouraged the MP for Rochdale, Jacob Bright, to support the repeal of the Acts. He agreed with the stand to gain equality of the sexes and spoke out in one particular case. In March 1870, a prostitute, Elizabeth Holt, was jailed for refusing to undergo the medical examination required by law. Probably influenced by the views of the PRA and Elizabeth (Wolstenholme, not Holt!), Bright spoke up in the House of Commons by appealing to the Home Secretary:

> Elizabeth Holt is now ... a prisoner in Maidstone Gaol because she declined to subject her person to the fortnightly inspection of a surgeon; and, whether her refusal or the refusal of any woman to submit to this outrage would be followed by repeated periods of imprisonment so as to amount practically to perpetual incarceration?[3]

Elizabeth recruited men who had a public voice to speak out for the rights of women. She had also extended her network, and Jacob Bright continued to support her in future campaigns.

Elizabeth was a watchdog with a broad brief, and the PRA challenged other proposed legislation that was seen as restricting the rights of individuals. This included the Criminal Law Amendment Act (1871), which placed restrictions that banned picketing, and the Pedlars Act (1871), which introduced a very narrow definition of the term 'pedlar' that might restrict the work of travelling sales folks. Interestingly, this still applies today only now the monitoring of the Act includes the use of CCTV in many towns and cities.

Women's Emancipation Union

The winter of 1890–91 was a hard one for Elizabeth as she was suffering from ill health. However, the spring brought some good news with the judicial ruling on the Clitheroe case Regina v Jackson (see Chapter 5), which ruled in favour of the wife.

This spurred Elizabeth into action once more. She wrote to her friend, Harriet McIlquham, that she regarded it as a greater victory than the passing of the Married Women's Property Act. This result was probably the fillip she needed after a bout of ill health; it gave her fresh energy and restored her drive to take forward the cause of women's rights.

With her belief in the power of the pen, she wrote a series of letters to the *Manchester Guardian*. In one, she stated:

> *Of the momentous character of this judgement there can be no question. It is a declaration of law which is epoch-making in its immediate consequences, and its ultimate results reach far into the future, involving indeed the establishment of a higher morality of marriage, and the substitution in the relation of husband and wife, of the ethics of justice and equality for the old and worn-out code of master and slave.*[4]

The letters were published as a pamphlet asking for the support of people who wished to engage with legal and social reforms. This led a flood of financial support that Elizabeth used to set up the Women's Emancipation Union (WEU).

The WEU concentrated its resources and energies on encouraging women's participation in local government, both as voters and as candidates. Although by this time there were several organisations working in the field of women's rights, the WEU stood alone in making a strong link between the rights of a married woman over her own person and the pursuit of full citizenship.

The aims of the WEU clearly stated that women were due equality of rights and duties with men in all matters affecting the service of the community and the state. They should also have the opportunity for self-development by education in schools and throughout life, and freedom of choice in careers in industry and in marriage and parental rights. The demands were forward looking and ambitious, setting out a vision that we could argue has not yet been fully achieved.

The WEU held its first national conference at the Midlands Institute, Birmingham, 24–25 October 1892. The report from this conference starts with a summary of its foundations and Elizabeth's role in its creation.

In April 1891, Mrs Wolstenholme Elmy addressed a series of letters to the Manchester papers explanatory of the full legal effect of the decision in the then recent Clitheroe Case and of the consequences flowing therefrom. These letters recited various stages of progress already achieved towards the emancipation of the wife from her legal position of thrall or chattel, and indicated further reforms still necessary to make marriage legally what a true marriage always is morally - the free, loving, companionship of equal souls, recognising no lordship or mastery on either side.[5]

The meeting reported on the first area of work undertaken in support of the Women's Disabilities Removal Bill, which Elizabeth had contributed to drafting, to ensure that it included married women. The report emphasised that, although this was an initial area of work, the WEU was not solely a suffrage society. The Bill had been debated in the House of Commons in 1892 and was defeated by about twenty votes – a close call.

By seeking equality, this Bill was similar to the Equal Rights Amendment (ERA) in the USA that was passed by Congress in 1972 but failed to be ratified in 1982; it was finally ratified in the twenty-first century. The ERA campaign involved many courageous women such as Gloria Steinem.

The ERA is a proposed amendment to the United States Constitution designed to guarantee equal legal rights for all American citizens, regardless of sex. It seeks to end the legal distinctions between men and women in matters of divorce, property, employment and other matters. Clearly the WEU and their supporters were ahead of the USA in vision, if not in law.

Back to Victorian England, where the WEU was disbanded in 1899. Despite the organisation surviving fewer than ten years, it achieved a great deal. It held more than 150 meetings and engaged women in activism and in writing letters; more than 7,000 people received WEU correspondence.

The ERA campaign in the US used similar methods; watching the television programme *Mrs America* gives us some sense of the physical effort of writing and putting so many letters into envelopes. Both campaigns needed women of stamina and determination, as well as courage since many of them faced physical threats.

The WEU was significant in the way it influenced the

fight for the vote at the dawn of a new century. Although it never encouraged physical violence, it certainly laid the foundation for active militancy that was taken up by the younger generation of suffragists – which leads us into a discussion about women, the vote and the suffragettes.

Chapter 7: Suffragist to Suffragette

Force-feeding, police playing cat and mouse,* window smashing, women chaining themselves to railings: these are many of the familiar images associated with the militant actions of the suffragettes. However, they came after a long, peaceful and frustrating campaign by suffragists. Elizabeth was engaged in both campaigns: she was there from day one.

What was the difference between the suffragists and the suffragettes? Fundamentally, the suffragists were peaceful, whereas the suffragettes undertook militant action. Although it does not align with how Elizabeth would have expressed it, Sylvia Pankhurst described the difference as:

> The suffragists were ever prone to look upon their cause as a side issue and to apologise for any impatient attempt to press it to the front. The suffragettes, on the other hand, were ready to stake their all upon it and constantly proclaimed it to be the highest and greatest in the world.[1]

Today, all British citizens over the age of eighteen (unless subject to legal incapacity) have the basic human right to

---

* The Cat and Mouse Act became law in April 1913. It allowed for the release of suffragettes on hunger strike until they were strong enough to be taken back into prison and force-feeding could continue.

vote and have a voice in the democratic process. This right is the result of a hard-fought battle that brought physical suffering (and even death) to those involved. The suffrage campaigners struggled against opposition from both Parliament and the general public before eventually gaining full equal rights to vote in 1928.

Sylvia Pankhurst recognised that Elizabeth played a vital and sustained role in the fight for female emancipation. Although the name Pankhurst is now synonymous with gaining the vote, two generations of that family have acknowledged Elizabeth's efforts.

She was a key player in founding the suffrage movement. As the years progressed and both the Conservative and Liberal governments failed to grant women the vote, she transferred her allegiance from the more peaceful suffragists to the militant suffragettes.

The campaign for female emancipation is recognised as starting in the 1860s. However, as we have seen, women were writing about this back in the eighteenth century, and it was certainly part of women's demands at Peterloo and other large gatherings in the early nineteenth century.

An overview of the fight for the vote

Under Tudor and Stuart law, women who owned land had the vote in parliamentary elections; however, this right fell into disuse in the eighteenth century and a long hard fight was needed to win it back.

There were calls for the vote for women at Peterloo in 1819. In the same year, large meetings such as the one in Hunslet, Leeds, called for electoral reform. This small flame was fanned in 1831 when the *Westminster Review* published two articles on the topic; however, they soon changed their focus to arguing for full enfranchisement for men.

The Reform Act of 1832 extended the vote for men, but clearly stated that the vote was for the male person, thus unequivocally excluding women in a way that had never been specified before in English law. As a result of successive Reform Acts, by the end of the nineteenth century most men met the legal criteria to vote in both local and national elections.

For many women, the fight was about more than the parliamentary vote or improving laws relating to the general condition of women; their aim was to improve human rights by altering male behaviour and redefining relationships between men and women. In a radically changing society, this focus was the foundation of Elizabeth's work.

As women won concessions that created possibilities for them outside the domestic sphere, they became more aware of being denied political rights. Furthermore, some of the laws that Elizabeth fought against illustrated the need for the female voice in Parliament. As Mary Dilke wrote in the *Women's Suffrage Journal* in 1885:

> If women had possessed votes during former administrations, undoubtedly the Contagious Diseases Acts would not have been imposed without a struggle, and the Factory Acts would have been submitted to a more thorough and impartial criticism.[2]

Women demanding the vote were challenging the order of the day and the widely accepted divide between the public and private spheres; consequently, many people (including politicians) regarded their demands with horror.

Over the years, women from different backgrounds joined the fight for the vote. Not surprisingly, there were differences of opinion and disagreements, largely about how to approach the campaign. What united them was the fundamental belief that women had the right to vote.

The differences of opinion resulted in the forming and disbanding of many different societies over the long period of this fight. Men were welcomed as members of some of these societies, and there were two organisations specifically for them. Most of the societies were not aligned to a political party because both parties failed to support the cause. The last society to be formed was the National Union for Equal Citizenship (1919–1928) which continued the fight until universal suffrage was won in 1928.

Many women, including Elizabeth, wielded the pen very effectively to present their arguments. One of the first leaflets was produced by Anne Knight, who also campaigned passionately against slavery. Harriet Martineau took up both these causes; she was one of the earliest female lead writers on a newspaper and had been appointed by Charles Dickens, who owned the *Daily News*.

From the 1860s onwards, many societies published their own pamphlets and journals. Barbara Bodichon established the *English Women's Journal* and Lydia Becker edited the *Women's Suffrage Journal*. These examples from the two journals[3] show that one presented a philosophical argument while the other outlined the action that women could take.

a) From the editorial of the *English Women's Journal:* The Enfranchisement of Women. Published 1 July 1864

Thus, many persons think they have sufficiently justified the restrictions on women's field of action, when they have said that the pursuits from which women are excluded are unfeminine, and that the proper sphere of women is not politics or publicity, but private and domestic life. We deny the right of any portion of the species to decide for another portion, or any individual for another individual, what is and what is not the proper sphere. The proper sphere for all human beings is the largest and highest which they are able to attain.

b) Speech delivered by Lydia Becker at a conference in January 1879 (subsequently reproduced in the *Women's Suffrage Journal*)

Men in this country obtained parliamentary representation in and through local government. They used the power they had, and they obtained more extended power. We urge women to follow their example – to take an interest in the local affairs in which they have a legal right to be represented*, to make their votes felt as a power which must be recognised by all who govern such affairs, and to be ready to fill personally such offices...

Throughout the suffrage campaign, politicians from the two major political parties held radically different views. Some argued that women were inferior and therefore unfit to vote; others argued that women's interests were the same as men's so they should be adequately represented.

Lydia Becker challenged these arguments as illogical. If women were inferior, that made them different to men so

---

* Municipal franchise for women was granted in 1869 to single, rate-paying women and gradually extended over the following three decades they needed representing. If, however, their interests were the same, there was no harm in granting them the vote.

Both Conservative and Liberal politicians fought against votes for women, although they did grant women a vote in local elections; some saw this as playing to women's roles in philanthropy. Herbert Asquith, a politician from 1886 and Prime Minister from 1908 to 1916, frequently blocked bills that aimed to give the vote to women, as did Gladstone.

The 1870 Suffrage Bill was supported by many councils, including the Manchester City Council, as well as with petitions that had more than 130,000 signatures. It seemed destined to give women the vote; the first reading was carried by more than one hundred votes. However, Gladstone, the Liberal Prime Minister, stepped in to ensure its subsequent defeat. When Jacob Bright introduced a bill the following year, Gladstone also manipulated its defeat. This pattern was repeated by Disraeli when he became Prime Minister.

Queen Victoria supported these politicians who objected to votes for women. Despite holding a position of power, the Queen was strongly opposed to female emancipation, as this declaration in 1870 shows.

The Queen is most anxious to enlist everyone who can speak or write to join in checking this mad, wicked folly of 'Women's Rights', with all its attendant horrors, on which her poor feeble sex is bent, forgetting every sense of womanly feelings and propriety. Feminists ought to get a good whipping. Were women to 'unsex' themselves by claiming equality with men, they would become the most hateful, heathen and disgusting of beings and would surely perish without male protection. [4]

From the earliest days, men such as Richard Pankhurst, John Stuart Mill and Jacob Bright supported the cry for emancipation. The campaigners, including Elizabeth, frequently encouraged these politicians to present bills to Parliament, but it was forty-eight years from the first Women's Suffrage Bill to the passing of the famous Representation of the Peoples Act in 1918.

A fight for half the nation

Elizabeth believed that half the nation was powerless and voiceless without the vote; this belief, alongside her many other campaigns for women's rights, was fundamental to her life's work.

During the 1865 general election, John Stuart Mill championed the call for women to have the vote and Barbara Bodichon supported his campaign. Elizabeth travelled from the north to London in July to hear him speak. She soon translated his words into action; a few months later she set up the Manchester Committee for the Emancipation of Women. She was joined by Josephine Butler, Lydia Becker, and Jacob and Ursula Bright, and they met in a house in Manchester's Upper Brook Street.

Sylvia Pankhurst,[5] who wrote about Elizabeth's pioneering work for women's rights from 1866, acknowledges that it is debatable if this was the first such group because records have been lost, but no one denies that Elizabeth was there at the start of the fight for the vote.

As soon as he became an MP, Stuart Mill set Bodichon the challenge of collecting one hundred signatures to support emancipation and promised to present the petition to the House of Commons. The new group got to work and excelled by collecting more than 1,000 signatures, of which Elizabeth was responsible for gathering more than 300. The national suffrage campaign was up and running; despite setbacks, it would continue until success was finally achieved.

Unfortunately, the size of the petition did not change the position of women. The 1867 Second Reform Bill extended the vote for some men but completely ignored women. That led to increased pressure on MPs through petitions and pamphlets.

In 1867, Lydia Becker wrote a paper advocating women's suffrage based upon their right to give expression to their political opinions through the ballot box. Recognising Elizabeth's power with the pen, Emily Davies sent the paper to her and asked her to use it as the basis for a report. According to Sylvia Pankhurst, who was clearly impressed by Elizabeth's work ethic, more than 10,000 copies were made.

In 1870 Jacob Bright brought the first Women's Suffrage Bill before Parliament, claiming that words relating to the masculine gender should always be seen as including women in this context. The hard work of the women campaigners and their supporters resulted in a similar Bill being introduced each year of the decade apart from 1875. Sadly, each one was defeated and the hard work continued.

Elizabeth left teaching in 1871, moved to London and took up her paid role as secretary with the PRA. She was now close to Westminster; she could maintain regular contact with MPs who supported women's suffrage, and challenge those who were opposed to a change in the law.

During this time, Elizabeth liaised closely with Jacob Bright MP, his wife Ursula, and his two sisters, who supported her work to repeal the CDAs and gain the vote. Sadly, Jacob Bright's more famous brother, John, was a radical MP and yet fiercely opposed women's vote. Divisions within a political family probably led to heated discussions over the dining table.

All the campaigners were busy throughout the 1880s and 1890s as their demands went unheeded by government. Differences emerged between the suffrage societies; some were prepared to accept a partial change in the law that allowed some women to vote, while Elizabeth and many others remained adamant that the law should give the vote to *all* women.

By the 1880s, this difference in principle was splitting the movement. Millicent Fawcett and Lydia Becker parted company with Elizabeth, probably after some heated debates, and no doubt this contributed to the creation of the Women's Franchise League (WFL).

In her book *Suffragette Movement: an intimate account of the persons and ideals*, Sylvia Pankhurst described how a small circle of ladies gathered in the bedroom of her mother, Emmeline Pankhurst, to congratulate her on the birth of her youngest son, Harry. Congratulations given, talk soon turned to how incensed they were at the continued support by some suffrage societies for excluding married women from the vote. This led to the formation of the Women's Franchise League (WFL).

The council of the new society included both Elizabeth and Ben, Jacob Bright and Josephine Butler, all people who had worked together tirelessly for years. The WFL was based on the key principle that women, whatever their marital status, should have the right to vote in all elections. It was this principle that Elizabeth held dear; she was not prepared to collaborate with those who sought to gain the vote for only some women.

The inaugural meeting of the WFL was held in London on 25 July 1889, and was addressed by William Lloyd Garrison, an American journalist, social reformer, suffragette and anti-slavery campaigner. He gave a lively speech.

The report of the inaugural meeting included an address by Dr Richard Pankhurst, which emphasised the WFL's principle of equal citizenship and their work to achieve this in the Women's Electoral Bill of 1889. He praised Elizabeth, stating that she had earned herself an historic place in the fight for female enfranchisement. Certainly she had played a fundamental role in creating the first suffrage society that specifically demanded the inclusion of married women.

Despite her role in founding this society and in its early work, Elizabeth's feisty nature soon came to the fore. Following personal disagreements and philosophical differences, she resigned in July 1890. On a personal level, life was hard for her at this point and she considered stepping away from campaigning; however, a few months later she was back fighting for change.

After a hard winter, she was pleased to hear the positive outcome of the Clitheroe Case. As we've already seen, Regina v Jackson heard in favour of the wife. This outcome stirred up much public debate and was covered in newspapers as far afield as Australia.[*] Elizabeth's letters to the *Manchester Guardian* generated the funds to establish

---

[*] The Argus, Melbourne, 30 May 1891.

the Women's Emancipation Union (WEU).

As previously discussed, the WEU was certainly radical. Elizabeth believed passionately that the laws of the country should not force women to be submissive and passive; they should have control over their bodies, even in the marital bed. The WEU linked this to the fight for the vote; it was the only suffrage society to link the vote to challenging the doctrine of feme coverture, where a woman lost her status as feme sole upon marriage, and thus her right to own property.*

The society's approach was to create collaboration between classes and to seek mixed-sex membership. One strategy was to engage working-class women and encourage them to value their dignity and worthiness and stand up for their rights. More of them became involved and joined both the emerging trade unions for women and the suffrage groups. Thus, we get the images of women leaving the mills to spend hours walking narrow alleys and courtyards collecting signatures and firing up more women to call for change. The WEU laid the foundations of women's rights for working-class women and of the militancy that came to the fore with the upcoming generation of suffragettes.

Despite its achievements, the society's finances took a sharp decline when the 1897 Women's Franchise Bill failed, and by 1899 it had to close. Elizabeth wrote a paper that summarised the WEU's work and offered a conclusion that can still speak to us today as people who have lived

---

* Upon marriage, a woman, became a feme coverture, meaning that her legal rights and obligations passed to her husband. As we have seen, Elizabeth had been fighting this with some success for many years.

our lives in ways strongly influenced by the suffragists and suffragettes. She stated that:

> They who inherit the labour of others, endeavour to pay their debt to the past by labour for the present and the future, assured that not even a wish for good is ever utterly wasted, but bears somewhere and somehow fruit after its own kind. To this effort for truth and justice, and for progress of the race, they earnestly invite everyone who has profited, or may yet profit, from the bygone labours of the WEU.[6]

Let's get militant – deeds not words.

At the start of the new century, with a new king on the throne[*] there was still the same old resistance by politicians to female emancipation. The years of failure frustrated Elizabeth to the point where her views shifted and became more radical; like many younger activists, she was coming to see militant action as the way forward.

Elizabeth was now approaching seventy but was relentless in her determination to make democracy available to all women. Such a radical view raised the possibility of mass political protest, thus laying the foundation for the suffragette movement; it also introduced methods that are still used worldwide today.

If one event marked the change in Elizabeth's stance, it was the meeting held at Mowbray House, London, on 8 May 1903. Many who attended were probably expecting a genteel suffrage meeting but what they got reframed their thinking

---

[*] King Edward VII came to throne after his mother, Queen Victoria, died on 22 January 1901.

and refashioned the whole movement. Just imagine the chat afterwards over a cup of tea – or something stronger!

William T. Stead introduced Elizabeth as the principal speaker and helped her onto a chair so that she could be seen. Epic in ideas and passionate in her views, she was nevertheless diminutive in stature! Her speech clearly demonstrated the shift in her views. Back in 1865, she had called for the vote for women as a route to help them serve the nation; in 1903, she was demanding the vote for women, using the right to revolt if necessary. She wanted full emancipation for all women.

Demonstrating her breadth of reading and intellectual ability, she referred to the physical frailty of army recruits (reported from the recently ended Anglo-Boer War) and made a direct link between their state and the despairing state of working-class mothers. Part of the problem, she argued, was that women were legally unable to refuse sexual intercourse with husbands, so they could not protect their health, limit family size and raise robust, physically fit children.

She was supported in this by Stead, who said that women needed the legal right to control family size; this, in turn, would strengthen the health and fabric of society. These were ideas that many of the female listeners had not heard before, certainly not spoken publicly in a large meeting; they would have to judge carefully with whom they could share them – probably not with their husbands!

Later, Stead regarded this meeting at Mowbray House as significant in the shift towards militant activism. He viewed Elizabeth as the brains of the movement, an opinion supported by the Pankhursts.

As so often with Elizabeth, her words then informed her actions. Cooperating with Stead and members of the NUWSS, she regularly travelled to London over the coming months to play a key role in organising the National Convention in Defence of Civil Rights of Women held at Holborn Town Hall. Dora Montefiore stated that it was this meeting that put the increasingly inert suffragist movement on the road to militant activity.

Other significant events occurred in late 1903. The Independent Labour Party was refusing to allow women to join, something that infuriated Emmeline Pankhurst, especially as they met in the Pankhurst Hall that had been built in memory of her beloved husband Richard,* who had fought long and hard for the suffrage movement.

Following on from this, a meeting of women with Emmeline and Christabel led to the creation of the Women's Social and Political Union (WSPU). To ensure there was no affiliation to political parties, this was to be a women-only society focused solely on gaining the vote for women; its motto was 'deeds not words'. As Elizabeth turned seventy, her passion for this cause found her willing and able to join the group and bring her tenacity to the fight.

In May 1905, Blackford Slack MP introduced a suffrage bill. Was seventy-year-old Elizabeth at home in Congleton with her feet up? No, she was in London supporting the WSPU by haranguing MPs as they passed through the central lobby of the House of Commons.

The experience energised her, and she fully supported Emmeline who called for an impromptu meeting outside when the Bill was talked out. The police were not in favour

---

* Dr Richard Pankhurst died in Manchester in July 1898.

of this meeting.

Each time Elizabeth rose to speak, the police moved them on; each time she started speaking, the group reconvened to hear her. The Labour leader Keir Hardie persuade the police to allow the meeting to take place outside Westminster Abbey – and he personally escorted Elizabeth there. Once the group assembled, they agreed on a resolution of indignation against the government. Emmeline Pankhurst later described this unauthorised gathering as the first militant action of the suffragette movement.

Elizabeth admitted to her friend Harriet McIlquham that she was tired but happy with the outcome of the day. Two years later, she told Sylvia Pankhurst that she had hoped to go to prison that day because she had come to believe that going to prison – and even dying – would be necessary to win the vote. Sadly, her fears proved true over the coming years.

On 19 May 1906, Elizabeth was in a deputation of women in a crowded room in the Foreign Office. Emily Davies presented the case supported by suffragists, co-operators, temperance workers and socialists, and Emmeline Pankhurst gave the closing address. The Prime Minister, Campbell-Bannerman, expressed support but encouraged patience since not all members of the Cabinet were in support. Keir Hardie countered this with a comment about patience being carried too far. Elizabeth added the reminder that she had worked for the cause since 1865. How much patience was needed? Clearly, a great deal.

In October, she travelled to London to take up a seat on the national executive of the WSPU and to attend another Westminster demonstration. This time ten women were arrested; Elizabeth had anticipated this but was disappointed that she wasn't amongst them. It seemed that the police were avoiding arresting older women.

Undeterred, the next day she presented herself at Westminster Police Court and asked to be listed as a witness; instead, she was locked in an anteroom with other demonstrators. Later that week she wrote to the *Manchester Guardian* accusing the police of brutality.

In June 1908, Elizabeth was in London again, this time to attend a huge suffragette demonstration. On that hot sunny day, she walked from Euston Station to Hyde Park, accompanied by Emmeline Pankhurst and carrying a bouquet of purple and white flowers with green ferns to represent the suffragette colours. At this event, the younger activists formally acknowledged her work on women's rights and named her 'nestor', or sage, of the suffrage movement.

Later that year she attended more demonstrations around the country, including one in Heaton Park, Manchester. She was frequently presented with flowers in the suffragette colours. Elizabeth had been fighting for women's rights for more than forty years and experienced much criticism; finally, she was being praised and seen as a heroine.

In 1908, Emmeline Pankhurst and others were arrested for smashing windows* and other violent deeds. In her defence, she explained that the aim of the WSPU was not to be law breakers but law makers. Elizabeth had sown the seeds for such action and, because of the inaction of both political parties, believed that militancy was the way

---

* Of all the women present that day, Victoria Liddiard lived the longest. She died aged 102 in 1992.

forward. However, she withdrew briefly when the violence escalated. From July 1912 to early 1913, the suffragettes sent some MPs letter bombs and even undertook bomb attacks; in February 1913, a bomb exploded in the summer house of David Lloyd George.[*]

By June 1913 Elizabeth was back, writing that the blame for law breaking lay with the government and their denial of the rights of citizenship by failing to give women the vote. Later that year, suffragette supporters and racegoers witnessed Emily Wilding Davies being crushed to death at the Derby in June 1913; she was trying to attach the suffragette colours to the King's horse when she was struck and killed.

Despite her shift towards militant action, Elizabeth maintained her links with the suffragist NUWS. In July 1913, more than 50,000 suffragists, dressed in their colours of red, white and green, converged in Hyde Park, London. This was the culmination of the Women's Suffrage Pilgrimage when women came from all over the country. Many of them had walked for up to six weeks, stopping in towns to give speeches at large open-air events. Even the suffragists were adopting more active forms of campaigning.

Between 1913 and 1918, the world changed beyond all recognition as the Great War ravaged lives. In support of the country, many women laid aside their fight for the vote and accepted roles and responsibilities previously denied them. Clearly, this played an important role in changing the mind of politicians.

Elizabeth was eighty-four when the Representation of the People Act, 1918, granted the vote to all women over

---

[*] He was Chancellor of he Exchequer at the time.

the age of thirty. The age condition was largely to maintain the dominance of male voters; due to the terrible loss of life during the war, giving equal rights would have resulted in there being more female voters than male. Full equal rights to vote would have to wait for another ten years.

◆ ◆ ◆

Should half the population have the right to play their part in the democratic processes of a country? The words and deeds of many thousands of women and men showed that they should. A few of them stand out for their personal dedication and suffering for the cause, and Elizabeth is one. She never stopped believing that women should have the vote. One can only imagine what she said when she was told on her deathbed that the 1918 Act was law.

Chapter 8: The Congleton Years

Elizabeth lived most of her adult life in Congleton, Cheshire, from where she regularly travelled around the country pursuing her commitment to change the world for women.

After working as a governess, Elizabeth moved back to Manchester to establish a school in Worsley. In May 1867, she relocated the school to Moody Hall in Congleton, where she worked full time until 1871.

It is not surprising that her reputation and experience led to the offer of headmistress posts in various notable schools. She refused these, closed her school in 1871, and relinquished the lease on Moody Hall. Although her dedication to education for females was as strong as ever, she could no longer handle the dilemma of teaching religious doctrine while holding secular views. In 1839, Sara Ellis had written that a female teacher should be dedicated to cultivating an understanding of religious principles; despite many changes since then, religious teaching was still a key part of any teacher's work.

Closing the school must have been a loss to the local community as well as to education in general, but it allowed Elizabeth to drive forward the cause of women's rights. As already discussed, she was soon invited to become secretary to the PRA. Her work with that organisation, and her many campaigns, meant she travelled regularly. When she went to school at Fulneck, she travelled by road. Now that major cities were connected by trains that could reach speeds of up to eighty miles an hour, she could travel much faster.

An additional benefit of the railways was that newspapers printed in London could be transported and sold 'hot from the press' in the provinces. Elizabeth, always keen to keep up to date with both national and international news, must have welcomed this.

With the growth of industry and business, cities became much busier. Dickens wrote in *Bleak House* of clogging smoke descending on people, along with black flakes of soot the size of snowflakes. Horses splashed passers-by with mud (and much worse) as they jostled through crowded streets. Dirt and poor hygiene were everywhere; in addition, there were pickpockets, prostitutes and men with advertising boards.* Although Congleton was industrial, Elizabeth must have found the conditions in the larger cities worse. This heightened her awareness of the desperate conditions in which many people lived and worked.

She frequently visited the House of Commons to listen to debates and harangue MPs who failed to support her petitions relating to women's rights. The Palace of Westminster had burned down in 1834, not long after Elizabeth's birth, and was rebuilt to the design of Augustus Pugin. Who could have imagined that the young Elizabeth would one day frequent it to fight for her beliefs?

---

* Street advertising started in the 1830s and Dickens coined the phrase 'sandwich board'.

A Ladies' Gallery was installed during the rebuild, complete with windows covered with heavy metal grilles that made it difficult to see or hear. Millicent Fawcett wrote that it was like wearing a gigantic pair of spectacles that didn't fit; it gave women headaches and made them feel like victims. The grilles were both a physical and metaphorical symbol of women's exclusion from Parliament.

Breaking down barriers

The first women campaigners are recorded in the 1830s. By boycotting slave-grown cotton and sugar, they got the term 'gradual abolition' dropped from the Anti-Slavery Society. Considering the political stance of Elizabeth's family, it is likely that she heard of this campaign when she was young and came to appreciate how power could be exerted by those who appeared to be powerless.

Throughout her adult life, Elizabeth moved outside accepted social norms and challenged traditional perceptions of women. Many early feminists were regarded as unfeminine. Women were still believed to be subservient in a male-dominated world, and many men strongly opposed them challenging power, be that in politics, business or the home.

Elizabeth and her allies were regarded as putting forward unacceptable radical ideas that challenged the law and religion, and many of them were prepared to speak openly in public. Elizabeth not only showed her strength of character by speaking openly in public and addressing mixed audiences, she went further by talking in mixed-sex groups about marital rape, a taboo subject that had never been publicly addressed.

As a result of her work in education, Elizabeth was one of the first women to testify before a Royal Commission. Over the coming years, other women followed in her footsteps by appearing before Royal Commissions and select committees. Such appearances gave them a way of pressurising Parliament despite having no formal power.

Power of the pen

Elizabeth could speak effectively but her real skill was expressing herself in writing, a skill enhanced by her sharp intellect, the breadth of her reading and her ability to weave together research, rational arguments and emotion.

She had read widely from childhood, so her writing often drew on research and the views of respected writers. Women's journals played an important role in sharing issues of women's rights; in July 1864, the editorial of the *English Woman's Journal** offered a clear argument that was closely aligned with Elizabeth's.

When a prejudice, which has any hold on the feelings, finds itself reduced to the unpleasant necessity of assigning reasons, it thinks it has done enough when it has reasserted the very point in dispute, in phrases which appeal to the pre-existing feeling. Thus, many people think they have sufficiently justified the restrictions on women's field of action, when they have said that the pursuits from which women are excluded are unfeminine, and that

---

* *English Woman's Journal*. Founded by two women whom Elizabeth worked alongside: Barbara Bodichon and Bessie Raynor Parkes.

the proper sphere of women is not politics or publicity,
but private and domestic life. We deny the right of any
portion of the species to decide for another portion, or
any individual for another individual, what is and what
is not a proper sphere. The proper sphere of all human
beings is the largest and highest to which they are able
to attain to.[1]

Elizabeth developed an unparalleled grasp of parliamentary procedures and demonstrated this skill when tackling a detailed piece of legislation or text by adding comments, facts and figures to support her arguments. A classic example is the paper she presented on 3 March 1880 to the Dialectical Society, where she demonstrated a thorough understanding of the Criminal Code Bill and analysed it in relation to women.

For example, she unpicked Section 181 that would, in her view, make any pregnant woman open to the charge of murder for failing to obtain assistance in childbirth. She highlighted that there was no definition of 'reasonable assistance', nor a clear time frame, so any woman, whatever her intent, could be held responsible for the murder or manslaughter of her child.

With a similar forensic analysis, she exposed the way the law upheld marital rape. She argued vociferously against this by stating that:

I submit that rape, being a violation of a primary natural
right is, and ought to be by law declared to be wholly
independent of any legal or other artificially created
relationship between the parties, and that it would be
a gross immorality to enact, as the section I have just
quoted proposes implicitly to do, that any such act, by a

husband, however base and cruel it may be, is justified by the matrimonial consent of the wife once given and never to be retracted.[2]

Her wide reading, attention to detail and ability to recall information were skills she applied often in her correspondence with friends, colleagues and opponents. Her stream of daily letters included useful information, newspaper cuttings and quotes from pamphlets and letters she had received, plus lists of how MPs had voted on particular bills. By sharing these, she provided the recipients with valuable information they could use in their own writing and public speaking.

Sometimes her letters to friends showed her feelings about the issues for which she was fighting. In the early Edwardian period, she wrote to her longstanding friend Harriet McIlquham about the need for a great effort to drive forward the call for the vote and expressed the opinion that many of them would not see it pass into law despite their long fight.

At one point, she was writing up to three hundred letters a day by hand; she was probably very grateful for a typewriter gifted to her by the cousin of Oscar Wilde. Luckily Buxton House, her home in Congleton, was next door to the post office!

In addition to letters, she wrote informative and passionate pamphlets, essays, poetry, reports, journal and newspaper articles. She and Ben published books together, particularly relating to sex education for children. She turned her pen to poetry, and her wide reading informed the lectures she gave at the Cooperative Hall in Congleton. In December 1893, she spoke about the poetry of Lord

Tennyson; the local newspaper described her talk as showing an enthusiastic appreciation of his work.

The range of her writing offered a wealth of material for a biographer. W.T. Stead intended to fulfil this role, and Elizabeth would probably have appreciated and supported him, but unfortunately he was one of the many passengers on the *Titanic* who lost their lives.

Sadly, it is recorded that several trips by a horse and cart during World War 1 removed Ben's papers from Buxton House; they were probably donated in response to the call for wastepaper. Less is known about the fate of most of Elizabeth's papers. She strongly believed in the importance of her work and may have been working on an autobiography. Perhaps it was the frail state of both her physical and mental health that, for once, prevented her pen from achieving its aim.

Elizabeth shared the power of the pen with thousands of other women by enabling them to sign petitions. She used these during almost every campaign she fought; they were a way to empower the powerless. Elizabeth took petitions to the mills as women left work, and in this way she played her part in politicising working women.

During the fight for the vote, one year stands out. In 1897, there were more than 1,200 petitions submitted to Parliament, with nearly 45,000 signatures. Petitions are still used today, and people can sign them using social media; in the nineteenth century, it took a phenomenal amount of physical work to prepare and collect the signatures. Elizabeth was involved directly in this work and will have understood the impact that petitions could have upon MPs.

Connections – her network and friendships

As a strong-minded, radical free-thinker, Elizabeth often placed causes before people. She stuck to her principles, sometimes in the face of significant disagreement, and occasionally friendships ended abruptly because of her intransigence. Despite this, her friendships were important to her, and her correspondence winged its way across the globe, connecting women from different cultures who were linked by their belief in women's rights.

Over the years, she built up a network that included many international activists. Some of them contributed to her developing feminism; in the 1890s, her thinking shifted more towards theories of citizenship and democracy.

It is also worth noting that Elizabeth placed women's rights issues before all other beliefs; that meant she could work effectively with women who were quite different to her in their religious beliefs, social standing and background. If they were the right people for a role, Elizabeth encouraged and supported them.

No doubt this was the case with Josephine Butler, who had a leading role in the fight against the CDA laws. Religion was important to Josephine throughout her life; her mother was a dedicated Moravian, descended from the Huguenots. Both Josephine and Elizabeth had been exposed to the principles of the Moravian faith and, although their beliefs later diverged, these principles are clear in how they worked together. Elizabeth, unlike Josephine, became a secularist in her adult life and turned against the church, partly due to its preaching on the position of women.

Barbara Bodichon was another example of a woman

who was quite different to Elizabeth in many ways. She was a recognised artist and married to a French philosopher. Despite their differences, Barbara's work for women's rights appealed to Elizabeth and she joined the Langham Group, which Barbara and others established. This group, and the related NAPSS, gave Elizabeth access to a varied network of associates that she drew on throughout her many campaigns.

At the age of twenty-one Barbara had stated views that would ring true with Elizabeth:

Philosophers and Reformers have generally been afraid to say anything about the unjust laws both of society and country which crush women. There never was a tyranny so deeply felt yet borne so silently, that is the worst of it. But now I hope there are some who will brave ridicule for the sake of common justice to half the world.[3]

Dora Montefiore was living in Australia when she lost her husband at sea and discovered she had no right to the guardianship of her children. This drove her to become an advocate for women's rights. Following a stay in Paris, she moved back to England where she built a long relationship with Elizabeth. She talked positively about Elizabeth and their friendship in her autobiography *Dora Montefiore: from a Victorian to a Modern* (Appendix 2).

Soon after her move to Congleton, Elizabeth met Ben Elmy, who became her lifelong partner and husband. She was still teaching, having opened Moody Hall as a school, while Ben had left teaching and bought a mill; like Elizabeth, he was opposed to the strong connection between education and religion. Ben Elmy was friends with Charles Bradlaugh, who became Vice President of the

National Secular Society, so it is unsurprising that he and Elizabeth became close associates.

At this point, personal life and principles clashed once more. Secularism was so important to Elizabeth that in July 1869 she refused to attend her brother's wedding. Although she invited the couple to Congleton and they married in the local church, St Peter's, she remained at home. If she had attended, she would have heard Theresa Kraus agree to obey her husband, Joseph Wolstenholme. Even though Elizabeth was fond of the couple, her principles would not allow her to go to the service.

Ben and Elizabeth worked together to establish the Congleton Ladies Education Society and later arranged talks. For example, Charles Bradlaugh helped them to arrange for Annie Besant, a women's right activist and atheist, to speak in Congleton. This raised more than a few eyebrows; once the topic was known, the event was banned from the Town Hall and rearranged at the Co-operative Society. At a talk in later years, stones were thrown and Elizabeth sustained a cut above her eye; despite such events, she and Ben remained faithful to their beliefs.

It was their belief in free love and secularism that led them to live together rather than take the accepted route of a wedding. Friends were prepared to ignore this arrangement until Elizabeth became pregnant. In the spring of 1874, the couple unwillingly responded to the outcry by having a simple ceremony with vows that ensured equality and freedom while recognising their shared love. Sadly, this was not enough for opponents who were concerned about the impact of their relationship upon the wider cause of women's rights. Thus, in October, they gave in to the pressure and held a civil ceremony at Kensington Registry Office.

Ben was furious that there had been such pressure. It is possible that among their friends this was the start of rumours about him being an inadequate husband; many of Elizabeth's friends strongly disliked him. Sylvia Pankhurst suggests that the stories reflected his feelings about the ceremony, followed by his writing about such taboo subjects as sex education. It is her view that, rather than him being unfaithful and cruel to Elizabeth, life was harsh due to their poverty and Elizabeth's workload.

Elizabeth always spoke tenderly of Ben. Sadly, their son, Frank, was frail and lacked his parents' drive, possibly due to the conditions of his upbringing – he grew up in poverty and with a mother who worked all hours. Even so, Elizabeth wrote with passion about the importance of the mother in childrearing, so one can assume that she was a caring mother.

Ben established Eaton Mills when he moved to Congleton and the silk production business was initially successful. It enabled him to demonstrate his principles by paying wages directly to female employees, which was highly unusual and unwelcome to many men. It was during the successful period of the mill that Elizabeth left London in 1875 and they moved to Buxton House. From then on, Buxton House became the centre of her many campaigns and was frequently used for meetings.

In September 1886, Elizabeth and Ben's lives changed dramatically. Cheap competition from abroad was already threatening the silk industry; this was followed by a disastrous fire that destroyed the four-storey mill. Unfortunately,

Ben did not have insurance, so the only option was to sell the property by auction in 1890.

They tried to save the business, with Elizabeth undertaking long hours of manual work, but to no avail. It is possible that weaving was done at Buxton House; there is clear evidence, both in the structure of the house and an old photograph, that at one time the first floor at the front of the house held a large loom. We don't know whether this was constructed before they bought Buxton House or following the mill fire, but it is likely that Elizabeth and Ben worked on it alongside the few workers they continued to employ. Sadly, despite this effort, the business folded.

With the sale of the mill went any financial security the family had known, especially as they continued to put what money they had into financing the campaigns, be that postage for petitions or travel for Elizabeth.

In addition to his own writing, Ben supported Elizabeth in her work, especially in setting up the Women's Emancipation Union. To support the finances of this organisation, he played a major role by mortgaging Buxton House. Clearly they both put work for women's rights well ahead of their personal situation.

Ben died in March 1906. Despite Elizabeth's care, he succumbed to bronchitis. His death was mourned by both Elizabeth and Frank and reported in various newspapers and journals, together with full accounts about the value of his work.

Naturally, the funeral proceeded without any religious ceremony as he would have wished. It is reported that he was cremated at Manchester; what is not reported, except in much later work by Sylvia Pankhurst, was that Elizabeth took his ashes out to sea to a point equidistant between England, Scotland and Ireland where she scattered them to the winds. Pankhurst says that three young suffrage friends accompanied her who she believed would continue the work she had started.

Throughout her adult life, Elizabeth suffered bouts of both physical and mental ill health. Her lifestyle and the pace at which she worked must have contributed to these, yet she remained passionate about women's rights to the end of her life.

Some members of Elizabeth's network recognised her financial difficulties as she grew older, but pride prevented her from accepting their support. Financial difficulties were never far from her door. She lived according to her beliefs and in pursuit of her principles; this frequently meant that life was challenging and finances were tight.

She often rose at three in the morning to work for up to eight hours on her political interests before undertaking domestic duties. This was partly because she could not afford servants, and, as many of the household devices we take for granted had not yet been invented, she had to do the washing, cooking and cleaning by hand.

Elizabeth continued to live at Buxton House in Congleton and only moved out following a fall down the stairs in which she sustained a head injury. On 12 March 1918, at the age of eighty-four, she died just six days after the law giving women the vote was passed. The *Manchester Guardian* reported that she lived long enough to hear the good news.

Pioneer or autocrat?

Some saw Elizabeth as a pioneer who drove forward the cause of women, while others regarded her as an impractical autocrat. Certainly, her radical lifestyle and sharp manner were sometimes unhelpful and partly explain these different reactions both during her life and afterwards. The relationships with the Pankhursts illustrates why she was airbrushed out of history.

Dr Richard Pankhurst collaborated with her from the early days of the campaigns, and many years later his wife, Emmeline, welcomed her contribution to the suffragettes. Their daughter, Sylvia, speaks highly of Elizabeth in her book published in 1911, yet her view had altered significantly by the time she wrote a history of the suffragette movement in 1931. This may have been because of a serious disagreement between Sylvia and her mother Emmeline.

In 1928, Sylvia became pregnant. She was not married; her mother was highly critical in public and accused her of following Elizabeth's example. This really hurt Sylvia, and her relationship with her mother did not survive. It is possible that Emmeline had always disapproved strongly of Elizabeth's lifestyle – she certainly let it be known that she did not approve of Ben.

The breakdown of the mother–daughter relationship hurt Sylvia to the extent that it changed her opinion of Elizabeth. However, we may conclude that her most honest view is expressed in her moving obituary, published in 1918:

When others faltered because the cause was unpopular and the goal seemed far away Mrs Elmy remained constant and steadfast, and accomplished an immensity of work ... Even in her extreme old age she rose during the small hours of the morning in order that all her housework and cooking for the day might be finished before nine a.m. in order that she might devote the rest of her time to toiling for the cause of women and progress... The women of to-day and tomorrow will never know how much they owe to her; but those of the younger generation who have been privileged to know her and work with her will not forget the inspiration which they derived from her selfless devotion to principle and keen, vigorous, and never pausing industry on the cause.[4]

Chapter 9: Elizabeth – a woman for women

Elizabeth was truly a woman who worked for women and contributed significantly to how ideas about them changed during the nineteenth century. Her life mirrored the emergence of various ideas that informed feminism, so it is worth examining the lessons that all feminists can take from her work.

Elizabeth's life and emerging feminism

According to some historians, three phases of feminism can be traced through the nineteenth century; these illustrate how Elizabeth was influenced by, and influenced, the changes that gradually transformed society.

In the 1820s to 1830s, when Elizabeth was born and grew up in the north of England, her family were committed to the radical politics associated with Manchester where they lived. As the city grew, so did the poverty of its workers. The Unitarian radicals, of which her family were very much a part, argued strongly that there was a clear connection between the subordinate legal status of women and their lack of political power. As a young girl, Elizabeth will have engaged in such debates as well as attending protest rallies.

Ironically, despite her family's views, she was denied the education she craved; this certainly fired her commitment to girls' education.

In the mid-nineteenth century, radicalism gave way to a focus on political, social and legal reforms. Although this was often driven by middle-class women, Elizabeth was a key player because of her determination and work ethic. She was at the front of the fight for the recognition of the sexual oppression of women in marriage.

During this period, more women became aware of language and how it was used to support male power; even now, there are concerns about the use of male pronouns to describe both men and women.

In 1868, a Manchester widow called Mrs Lily Maxwell went to vote at a local by-election because her name appeared on the voters' register. This was challenged in court and it was legally accepted that every woman was incapable of exercising a vote. Possibly spurred on by this, an article appeared in 1874 claiming that contact had been established with the planet Venus, where apparently all political business was conducted by females. The article went on to describe the horror of recent proposals that suffrage on Venus should be extended to men.

This no doubt rang true with many readers of the time, and still will for those who were into self-help books in the 1970s. *Men Are from Mars, Women Are from Venus* explored difficulties in relationships and communication between men and women – language challenges that still exist today.

Many of the self-help books of the late twentieth century and beyond have picked up the concept of 'imposter syndrome'. Did Elizabeth experience this? Certainly, many of the women she worked with during the mid-nineteenth century had stronger financial resources and, unlike Elizabeth, many of them upheld their religious beliefs. No doubt she felt an outsider at times, yet her beliefs and skills kept her passions alight, together with the support of her friends and Ben Elmy.

From the 1880s, there was a return to the radicalism of earlier times, although now it was connected to conditions for working women and linked women with the growing trade unions and the labour movement. Although Elizabeth experienced some hard times, she committed her energies to campaigning at mill gates, thus playing her part in radicalising working women. As the new century approached, she was prepared to adopt more militant action in the fight for the vote and, despite her age, continued to make a vital contribution to the ongoing battle for the rights of women.

As a young girl Elizabeth read Mary Wollstonecraft's *Vindication of the Rights of Woman* and she later acknowledged this text as influencing her thinking. By the middle of the Victorian period, the book had fallen into disrepute and the focus had moved to what was regarded as Wollstonecraft's scandalous life. As radical feminism emerged once more towards the end of the century and brought to the fore sexual freedom for woman, the book was regarded positively again, and Wollstonecraft was recognised as a founding figure of British feminism.

Looking forward

Over the years, feminism has continued to evolve as some rights have been gained and others have emerged. Having been denied the education she desired, Elizabeth fought tirelessly for girls' education; she would be impressed by current results, both in school exams and university degrees. However, behind the positive changes she probably noticed the barriers that females continued to face in certain fields of employment and pay.

The Equal Pay Act was not passed until 1970. To achieve this, women at a Dagenham car plant suffered weeks of strikes and gained the support of the Labour MP Barbara Castle, despite her facing opposition from many of her male left-wing Labour colleagues. Gaining women's rights always seems to come with suffering, a point clearly shown through Elizabeth's work.

In addition to changes in the workplace, the mid-twentieth century witnessed greater sexual freedom for women. Whereas many Victorian and Edwardian women had little understanding of the basic mechanics of intercourse, information was gradually becoming more available and encouraging women to enjoy sex. Elizabeth and Ben would have approved because of their aim to educate young people so that they could resist unwanted sexual advances. Elizabeth started campaigns against violence of all forms by men against women, including her daring discussion of marital rape. The laws on domestic violence have moved slowly; sadly, male violence towards women is still very topical.

Women held different views during the years that it took

to gain the vote, but they all agreed that women needed the vote and should be represented in the House of Commons. Although a few women entered politics, Lady Hale's memoir illustrates how slow progress has been. In 1966 only twenty-six of the 641 MPs were women; by 2019 this had risen to 220 out of 650. One imagines Elizabeth and her colleagues would be disappointed at such small numbers.

Lady Hale's work can be seen as building on Elizabeth's. As a member of the Law Commission, in 1971 she helped to introduce wide-ranging changes to divorce legislation. Interestingly, she comments upon the resistance to projects that would influence the division of property in cases of marital breakdown. The following quote is reminiscent of challenges faced by Elizabeth and her colleagues.

> ...the married men of the Lord Chancellor's Department did not expect to be divorced but neither did they expect to have to share ownership of their homes with their wives unless they wanted to.[1]

Changes *have* happened, and some may question the ongoing need for a feminist movement, but this view is clearly challenged by the Council for Europe

> There are people who believe that we do not need feminism today, but nothing could be further from the truth. Women have struggled for equality and against oppression for centuries, and although some battles have been partly won - such as the right to vote and equal access to education – women are still disproportionally affected by all forms of violence and by discrimination in every aspect of life.[2]

These few examples show that much has changed – and much remains to be changed. When appointed to UNESCO as Global Mentor for Gender Equality in 2008, Billie Jean King said:

> There is so much work still to be done when it comes to breaking down barriers to opportunity for women and girls throughout the world.[3]

Congleton celebrates

> To focus too exclusively on Elizabeth's part in the women's suffrage movement is ... to gloss over her true character – that of the humanist philosopher, who believed the possession of a human soul should alone guarantee to its custodian the rights of respect, honour and freedom.[4]

There were many in Congleton (and beyond) who opposed Elizabeth's views, yet she was acknowledged for her work in changing women's lives. Today there are still those who object to the way she chose to live, but she is now recognised and celebrated. In Congleton, the celebration is tangible; in the last few years, a new link road has been named after her, and a statue to mark her dedication to women's rights was unveiled on 8 March 2022.

Whatever our views about her personal life and beliefs, today we can celebrate the achievement of this amazing woman who changed our laws and laid the foundation for feminism in our world.

Lessons from Elizabeth

Elizabeth laid strong foundations for future generations to build upon. What can we learn from her achievements?

It is arguable that she put her causes before all else, sometimes at the expense of friendships and often at the expense of her home life and personal comfort. However, she was willing to adapt her thinking as the years progressed. Through the years of her campaigning, she demonstrated the ability to balance rational thought with emotive language both in her speeches and her writing.

She was renowned for her comprehensive knowledge and understanding of parliamentary procedures. She developed the ability to work with legal documents and reports to support her arguments. Others frequently benefited from her willingness to share material that she had spent hours compiling, enabling them to present detailed facts in their own speeches and articles.

During her youth in Manchester, she had seen at first-hand how the Anti-Corn Law League successfully fought their campaign. She never forgot the importance of rallies and petitions; the latter gave women the power to express their views to MPs, thus keeping them aware of the opinions of the unrepresented half of the population.

Elizabeth never gave up her fight for that half of the population. This brings us back to the opening question: was Elizabeth a feisty feminist?

The OED defines 'feminism' as the advocacy of women's rights on the grounds of equality of the sexes. What Elizabeth did ticks that box and more, so one can argue she was a feminist.

Was she feisty? If one accepts that as a positive description – of people who are dedicated to their beliefs and principles – then yes. However, language changes with the years and some people are less comfortable with the word now.

Was she a feisty feminist? That is for you to decide, but we can surely agree that she made a huge contribution to women's rights and paved the way for work that continues today.

Appendix 1: the timeline of a passionate feminist

1852–1854:   From the age of nineteen, worked as a governess in Luton.

1854–1871:   Headmistress of two girls' schools: Worsley, Manchester, and then Congleton.

1865:   Founded the Manchester Headmistresses' Association.

1866:   Set up the Enfranchisement of Women Committee.

1867:   Founded the North of England Council for promoting the education of women.

1867–1882:   Became Honorary Secretary of the Married Women's Property Committee.

1868:   Established the Ladies' Association for the repeal of the Contagious Diseases Act (these Acts were not repealed until 1886).

1871:   Formed the Committee for Amending the Law and Points Injurious to Women (soon renamed Personal Rights Association) and became the first employee of a women's rights movement.

The 1870s was a decade when Elizabeth and others prepared many suffrage bills and petitions.

1873:   The PRA and Elizabeth challenged Custody of Infants Act.

1874:	Started campaign against domestic violence.
1876:	Elizabeth was stoned by people in Congleton.
1880:	The PRA and Elizabeth challenged Guardianship of Infants Act.
1891–1899:	Responded to the Clitheroe case and founded the Women's Emancipation Union.
1903:	Elizabeth delivered a radical speech demanding the vote at Mowbray House, London. Speech seen as a game changer.
1906:	Ben Elmy died. Later that year, Elizabeth took an executive seat on the Women's Social and Political Union.
1907–1912:	Continued to be actively involved with both the suffragists and the suffragettes.

Appendix 2: Extract from Dora Montefiore: from a Victorian to a Modern.

Chapter 7: 'Militancy'

Mrs. Elmy, one of the most wonderful women who devoted her life and her intellectual powers to the cause of the emancipation of women, paid constant visits to London from her home in Cheshire, with the object of stirring up what seemed to be the dying embers of suffrage activities. She knew all the Members of Parliament who had at any time expressed in words, or who had helped with pen or with action our cause; and at the time of these visits to London (usually at the period of the promised debates in Parliament on a Suffrage Bill), she would visit these Members in the Lobby and do her best to stir them into action. The late Mr Stead, who was a great admirer of hers, would frequently help her to get up small private meetings of sympathisers and workers, and all of us who were looking for a lead in suffrage matters, welcomed these quaint and earnest appearances of hers in London, and derived encouragement from her experience of Parliamentary procedure and intense spiritual enthusiasm. She usually stayed at my house when she came to town, and I had the privilege of accompanying her when she interviewed Members of Parliament or other sympathisers. She must have been then between sixty and seventy, very small and fragile, with the brightest and keenest dark eyes and a face surrounded with little white ringlets. She was an old friend of and fellow worker with Josephine Butler and of John Stuart Mill, and in those days had been an habitué of what was then known as the "Ladies' Gallery" in the House of Commons. There, behind the grille, where they could see but not be seen by the Members of the House, these and other devoted women had sat night after night listening to the debates on the Contagious Diseases Acts, which raised questions that concerned their sex as much, if not more, than they did that of the men who were discussing them. This loyalty in the cause of their fellow-women who, they realised, suffered so severely under the C.D. Acts, brought them insult and opprobrium, but it also brought them many of the truest and most loyal friends that women ever possessed; and, as we know, the cause they stood for triumphed in the end.

My friendship with Mrs. Elmy and work with her continued during many years and our correspondence, between the periods of her visits to town, was continuous; I was keeping her au courant with what was going on in London, and she was interpreting, encouraging, sending me voluminous newspaper cuttings and helping forward my work in every way in her power with loving counsels and wisest advice. She never faltered in her belief that women's political enfranchisement was very near at hand, although, time and again, politicians betrayed and jockeyed us, while men who feared our influence in public life, insulted our efforts and talked out our Bills.

The longest terrace in Europe, it still exists today. From the Girls' School when Elizabeth was there, they could have come straight on to the terrace and then down the path to the gardens and Tong Valley.

Fulneck Church. The front of the Church is unchanged from the time that Elizabeth was attending services.

Images supplied by Fulneck Museum

Fulneck Shop. This would have been used by Elizabeth for exercise books and other materials. Today the same building is a café (Café 54) and is still well used by school pupils.

Buxton Road. This road runs from the centre of Congleton and is where Elizabeth and Ben lived together. It is along this road that she will have walked when returning from her many trips around the country.

Blue plaque. This appears outside the house on Buxton Road where Elizabeth and Ben lived.

Author's note: the blue plaque shows Elizabeth's date of birth as 1839; in fact she was born in 1833. The plaque was put up many years ago and is incorrect.

Image supplied by Congleton Museum.

Elizabeth at her desk in the home on Buxton Road.

Right: Elizabeth's statue in Congleton town centre.

Sculptor: Hazel Reeves.

Image supplied by Mary Evans Picture Library.

HYDE PARK DEMONSTRATION, SUNDAY, JUNE 21, 1908:
MRS. PANKHURST, MRS. WOLSTENHOLME ELMY.

Elizabeth with Emmeline Pankhurst on the Suffragette March in June 1908. Elizabeth had been given a large bouquet of flowers to mark her significant contribution to the campaign for the vote.

Endnotes

Introduction

1 Wolstenholme, Elmy (1885). Emancipation of Women. Quoted in Wright, Maureen (2011). *Elizabeth Wolstenholme Elmy and the Victorian feminist movement: the biography of an insurgent woman.* Manchester University Press. p. 153.
2 *Congleton* Chronicle. Thursday 31 August, 2006.
3 Ramelson, Marian (1972). *The Petticoat Rebellion: a century of women's rights.* London, Lawrence & Wishart. p. 52–53.

Chapter 1: Setting the scene

1 https://www.fawcettsociety.org.uk/about Accessed 07/10/2021
2 https://www.theguardian.com/news/2018/jan/04/peterloo-massacre-bloody-clash-that-changed-britain Accessed 07/10/2021
3 https://www.bl.uk/romantics-and-victorians/articles/the-peterloo-massacre Accessed 07/10/2021
4 Engels, Fredrich (1993). *The Conditions of the Working Class in England.* Oxford University Press.
5 https://www.britishnewspaperarchive.co.uk/search/results/1831-01-01/1862-12-31?basicsearch=preston%20procession&exactsearch=false&retrievecountrycounts=false&newspapertitle=manchester%20times Accessed 03/02/2021
6 Levine, Philippa. 'The Humanising Influences of Five o'clock Tea.' *Victorian Feminist Periodicals*, Victorian Studies. Winter, 1990, Vol. 33, No. 2. pp. 293–306
7 Atwood, Margaret. (2019). *The Testaments.* Penguin Random House, UK. p. 15.
8 https://www.bl.uk/romantics-and-victorians/articles/gender-roles-in-the-19th-century K Hughes. Accessed 07/10/2021

9 https://www.google.co.uk/books/edition/The_Subjection
_of_Women/kU4zAQAAMAAJ?hl=en&gbpv=
1&printsec=frontcover Accessed 05/02/2021
10 https://www.google.co.uk/books/edition/The_Duties_of_
Women/HZXDRIrKTLIC?hl=en&gbpv=1&printsec
=frontcover Accessed 06/02/2021

Chapter 2: The young life of a feisty feminist

1 Tyldesley, Bert (1993). *The duke's other village: the Roe
Green Story.* Roe Green Methodist Church (Internet version,
2000).
2 Rev Shawe, C.H. (1993). *The Spirit of the Moravian Church.*
Moravian Bookroom, London.
3 https://www.bl.uk/romantics-and-victorians/videos/the-
governess Hughes. K. Accessed 03/04/2021.
4 Wollstonecraft, Mary (1792). *A Vindication of the Rights
of Woman.* https://www.bl.uk/collection-items/mary-
wollstonecraft-a-vindication-of-the-rights-of-woman
Accessed 03/04/2021.
5 https://www1.britishnewspaperarchive.co.uk/search/
results/1848-05-18?NewspaperTitle=Bradford%2BObserver
&IssueId=BL%2F0000155%2F18480518%2F&County=Yor
kshire%2C%20England *Bradford Observer,* 1848. Accessed
05/04/2021

Chapter 3: The three 'Es'

1 Butler, J. Editor. (1869) *Woman's work and woman's culture:
a series of essays.* McMillan, London. Retrieved 24 February
2021, from https://books.google.co.uk/books?id=
mSUZAAAAYAAJ&printsec=frontcover&source=gbs_ge_
ummary_r&cad=0#v=onepage&q&f=false
2 Ellis, Sarah Stickney quoted (p. 24) in Phillip, Melanie
(2003). *The Ascent of Woman.* Warner Book, UK.
3 De Bellaigue, C. (2001). 'The Development of Teaching as a
Profession for Women before 1870.' *The Historical Journal,*
44, (4), pp. 963–988. Retrieved 8 February, 2021, from
http://www.jstor.org/stable/3133547

4 Ibid.

5 Wright, Maureen (2011). *Elizabeth Wolstenholme Elmy and the Victorian Feminist Movement: the biography of an insurgent woman.* Manchester University Press.

6 *Leeds Mercury.* Thursday 28 May 1868.

7 https://www.newn.cam.ac.uk/ Accessed 09/02/2021.

8 Butler J. (1868) quoted in Schwartz. L (Oct. 2011) 'Feminist Thinking on education in Victorian England.' *Oxford Review of Education,* 37, (5), pp. 669–682.

9 Davies. E. (2010). *The Higher Education of Women.* Cambridge University Press. First published 1866.

10 Bodichon, Barbara Leigh Smith. (1857). *Women and Work.* London. Retrieved 10 February, 2021 from https://www.bl.uk/collection-items/women-and-work

11 Beatrice Webb quoted in Thane, P (Autumn, 1978). 'Women and the Poor Law.' *History Workshop,* 6, p. 29, pp. 31–51. Retrieved 10 February, 2021, from https://www.jstor.org/stable/4288190

12 McCarthy, Helen (2021) *Double Lives: a history of working motherhood.* Bloomsbury.

13 https://futuresforwomen.org.uk/history/ Sourced 05/06/2021.

Chapter 4: Married life - heaven or hell?

1 https://intriguing-history.com/married-womens-property-act/ Sourced: 19/02/2021.

2 Shanley, Mary Lyndon (2021). *Feminism, marriage and the law in Victorian England,* 1850-1895. Bloomsbury Academic. Quoted page 159.

3 Phillips, M (2003). *The Ascent of Woman.* England

4 Quoted in Pankhurst, E. Sylvia (1931). *The Suffragette Movement: an intimate account of passions and ideals.* Longmans, Green & Co. pp. 48–49.

5 Ibid., p. 49

6 Wolstenholme, Elizabeth C. (1880). *The criminal code in relation to women.* A paper read before the Dialectical Society, March 3rd 1880. Manchester, Ireland & Co.

7 Shanley, Mary Lyndon. Quoted from p. 156.

8 Ibid.
9 Jerrard, R (1992). 'Marital Rape.' *Police Journal*, p. 340.
   Accessed: 19/06/2021. https://heinonline.org/HOL/
   LandingPage?handle=hein.journals/policejl65&div
   =54&id=&page=
10 Ryan, Rebecca M. (1995). 'The Sex Right: A Legal History
   of the Marital Rape Exemption.' *Law & Social Inquiry*,
   vol. 20, no. 4, 1995, pp. 941–1001. JSTOR, www.jstor.org/
   stable/828736. Accessed 19/06/2021.
11 http://icpdtaskforce.org/resources/2014-04-08-CPD2014-
   Navi-Pillay.pdf Accessed 19/06/2021.

Chapter 5: No sex please ... without equality

1 Wright, Maureen (2011). *Elizabeth Wolstenholme Elmy
   and the Victorian Feminist Movement: the biography of an
   insurgent woman.* Manchester University Press. p. 81.
2 Fischer, N (2018). *The Sovereign Body: Elizabeth
   Wolstenholme Elmy and the fight for women's autonomy.*
   Senior Thesis in the Department of History, Barnard
   College, USA. p. 23.
3 Waldron, J (2007). 'Mill on Liberty and on the Contagious
   Diseases Acts.' Ed. Nadia Urbinati & Zakaras, A. J.S. Mills,
   Political Thought: a bicentennial reassessment. Cambridge
   University Press. pp. 11–42.
4 Walkowitz, J.R. (1980). *Prostitution and Victorian Society:
   Women, Class and the State.* Cambridge University Press.
   Quoting Royal Commission of 1871 into the operation and
   administration of the CDAs.
5 Fischer, N (2018). *The Sovereign Body: Elizabeth
   Wolstenholme Elmy and the fight for women's autonomy.*
   Senior Thesis in the Department of History, Barnard
   College, USA. Quoting from Elizabeth Wolstenholme Elmy
   papers, British Library, London.
6 Hamilton, M. (1978). 'Opposition to the Contagious Diseases
   Acts, 1864-1886.' *Albion.* Cambridge University Press, (10) 1,
   pp. 14–27.

7 LNA, Annual Report for 1870 pp4 –5. Quoted in *Prostitution and Victorian Social Reform*. (1980). Paul McHugh. Croom Helm, London.
8 Fischer, N (2018). *The Sovereign Body: Elizabeth Wolstenholme Elmy and the fight for women's autonomy*. Senior Thesis in the Department of History, Barnard College, USA.
9 Ethelmer, Ellis (1893). *Woman Free*. London. p. 22.

Chapter 6: Watchdog with a bite

1 Personal Rights Pamphlet. Source: https://oll.libertyfund. org/page/personal-rights-association. Accessed 16/03/2021.
2 'Baby-Farming in Manchester.' Source: *The British Medical Journal*, Feb. 22, 1868, Vol. 1, No. 373 (Feb. 22, 1868), p. 174 Published by: BMJ. Stable URL: https://www.jstor.org/ stable/25213822
3 Wright, Maureen (2015). 'The perfect equality of all persons before the law: the Personal Rights Association and the discourse of civil rights, 1871-1886.' *Women's History Review*, Vol 24, Issue 1.
4 Elizabeth Wolstenholme Elmy letter to *Manchester Guardian*: quoted in Shanley, Mary Lyndon (1989). *Feminism, marriage and the law in Victorian England 1850–1895*. Princeton University Press.
5 The Women's Emancipation Union: its origin and its work: report presented at the inaugural meeting, held Birmingham, 24th October, 1892: with summarised report of the proceedings of the Conference, held Birmingham, 25th and 26th Oct., 1892. Source: JSTOR Primary Sources, 01-01-1892 Contributed by: Women's Emancipation Union. Stable URL: https://www.jstor.org/stable/10.2307/60223487

Chapter 7: Suffragist to suffragette

1 Pankhurst, E. Sylvia (1911). *The Suffragette: the history of the women's militant suffrage movement* 1905-1910. Gay & Hancock, London.

2 Mary Ashton Dilke: quoted in Levine, P. (1994) *Victorian Feminism (1850-1900)*. University Press of Florida.
3 Lewis, Jane. Editor. (1987). *Before the vote was won: arguments for and against women's suffrage*. Routledge & Kegan Paul. a) pp. 14–15. b) p. 349.
4 Abrams, Fran (2003). *Freedom's Cause: lives of the suffragettes*. Profile Books. p. xi.
5 Pankhurst, E. Sylvia (1931). *The Suffragette Movement: an intimate account of passions and ideals*. Longmans, Green & Co. p. 31.
6 The Women's Emancipation Union 1891-1899: an epitome of eight years effort for justice for women. Page 31 in original text. Accessed 04/05/2021: https://www.jstor.org/stable/60224025

Chapter 8: The Congleton years

1 Lewis, Jane Editor. (1987). *Before the Vote was Won*. Routledge & Kegan Paul, New York & London. pp. 14–15.
2 E.C. Wolstenholme Elmy (1880). 'The criminal code in its relation to women: a paper read before the Dialectical Society, March 3rd, 1880'. Manchester, 1880.
3 Hirsch, Pam (1998). *Barbara Leigh Smith Bodichon: feminist, artist and rebel*. Random House, London.
4 Wright, Maureen. *Elizabeth Wolstenholme Elmy and the Victorian feminist movement*. p. 237

Chapter 9: A woman for women

1 Brenda Hale (2021). *Spider Woman: a life*. The Bodley Head, London. p. 107.
2 https://www.coe.int/en/web/gender-matters/feminism-and-women-s-rights-movements
3 Bell, Jo, Hershman, Tania and Holland, Ailsa (2021). *On this Day She*. London. p. 107.
4 M Wright (2011). *Elizabeth Wolstenholme Elmy and the Victorian feminist movement*. p. 237.

Bibliography

Abrams, Fran (2003). *Freedom's Cause: lives of the suffragettes*. Profile Books.

Adiche, Chimananda Ngozi (2014). *We Should All Be Feminists*. (Audiobook).

Allende, Isabel (2020). *The Soul of a Woman*. Bloomsbury Circus, London.

Arnot, Margaret L. (1994). 'Infant death, child-care and the state: the baby-farming scandal and the first infant life protection legislation of 1872.' *Continuity and Change 9 (2)*. Cambridge University Press.

Atwood, Margaret. (2019). *The Testaments*. Penguin Random House, UK.

Banks, Olive & J.A. (1965). *Feminism and Family Planning in Victorian England*. Liverpool University Press.

Beard, Mary. (2018) *Women and Power, a manifesto*. Profile Books, London.

Bell, Jo, Hershman Tania and Holland, Ailsa (2021). *On this Day She*. Metro Publishing, London, UK.

Budd, S. (1977). *Varieties of Unbelief*. Heinemann, England.

Caine, Barbara (1992). *Victorian Feminists*. Oxford University Press.

Combs, Mary B. (2005). 'A Measure of Legal Independence: The 1870 Married Women's Property Act and the Portfolio Allocations of British Wives.' *The Journal of Economic History, Vol. 65, No. 4* (Dec., 2005). Cambridge University Press on behalf of the Economic History Association. Stable URL: https://www.jstor.org/stable/3874913. Accessed 07/06/2021

Davis, Philip. (2008). *Why Victorian Literature Still Matters.* Wiley-Blackwell.

De Bellaigue, C. (2001). 'The Development of Teaching as a Profession for Women before 1870.' *The Historical Journal, 44,* http://www.jstor.org/stable/3133547

Dodenhoff, Jenna. (2008). 'A dangerous kind: Domestic violence and the Victorian Middle Class.' *TCNJ Journal of Student Scholarship. Vol X*

Engels, Fredrich. (1993). *The Conditions of the Working Class in England.* Oxford University Press.

Frawley, Maria (1998). 'Emily Faithfull and 'The Victoria Magazine'.' *Victorian Periodicals Review.* Spring, 1998, http://www.jstor.com/stable/20083055

Forster, M. (1984). *Significant Sisters: Positive Feminism 1839-1939.* Secker & Warburg, London, UK.

Fraser, Antonia (2002). *The Weaker Vessel; Woman's Lot in Seventeenth-Century England, Part Two.* Clays, England.

Gaskell, Elizabeth Cleghorn (1997). *Ruth.* Penguin, London.

Hirsch, Pam. (1998). *Barbara Leigh Smith Bodichon: feminist, artist and rebel*. Random House, London.

Holcombe, Lee (1983). *Wives and Property*. Oxford, England.

Holton, Sandra Stanley. (1996). *Suffrage Days: Stories from the Women's Suffrage Movement*. Routledge, Oxon.

Holmes, Rachel (2020). *Sylvia Pankhurst: Natural Born Rebel*. Bloomsbury, London.

Houghton, Walter E. (1957). *The Victorian Frame of Mind: 1830-1870*. Yale University Press, New Haven and London.

Levine, Philippa (1994). *Victorian Feminism: 1850-1900*. University Press of Florida.

Lewis, Helen (2020). Difficult Women: a history of feminism in 11 fights. Jonathan Cape, London.

Lews, Jane (1991). *Women and social action in Victorian and Edwardian England*. Aldershot, England.

Lewis, Jane Editor. (1987). Before the Vote Was Won. Routledge & Kegan Paul, New York & London.

Liddington, Jill (2006). *Rebel Girls: Their Fight for the Vote*. Virago Press.

McCarthy, Helen. (2020). *Double Lives: a History of Working Motherhood*. Bloomsbury, London.

Nsaidzedze, Ignatius (2017). 'An Overview of Feminism in the Victorian Period [1832–1901].' *American Research Journal of English and Literature*. Volume 3, Issue 1

Pankhurst, E. Sylvia (1931). *The Suffragette Movement: an Intimate Account of Passions and Ideals*. Longmans, Green & Co.

Pankhurst, E. Sylvia (1911). T*he Suffragette: the History of the Women's Militant Suffrage Movement 1905–1910*. Gay & Hancock, London.

Purvis, Jane & Hannam, June. Editors. (2021). *The British Women's Suffrage Campaign*. Routledge, Oxon.

Ramelson, Marian (1972). *The Petticoat Rebellion: a Century of Women's Rights*. London, Lawrence & Wishart.

Richardson, Sarah (2018) 'Conversations with parliament: women and the politics of pressure in nineteenth-century Britain.' *Parliamentary History, 37 (Supplement 1)*.

Robinson, Jane. (2018). *Hearts and Minds: the Untold Story of the Great Pilgrimage and How Women Won the Vote*. Doubleday, London.

Roberts, M. J. D. (1995). 'Feminism and the State in later Victorian England.' *The Historical Journal, 38, 1* (1995)

Royale, E. (1980). *Radicals, Secularists and Republicans*. Manchester University Press, England.

Shanley, Mary Lyndon (1982). '"One Must Ride behind": Married Women's Rights and the Divorce Act of 1857.' *Victorian Studies,* Spring, 1982, Vol. 25, No. 3. Indiana University Press

Shanley, Mary Lyndon (1989). *Feminism, Marriage and the Law in Victorian England 1850–1895*. Princeton University Press.

Stapleton, A. Rev. (2008). *Memorials of the Huguenots in America*. Heritage Books.

Treasure, Geoffrey. (2013). *The Huguenots*. Yale University Press, New Haven and London.

Tusan, Elizabeth Michelle. (2000). 'Not the ordinary Victorian Charity: The Society for Promoting the Employment of Women.' *History Workshop Journal*. Spring 2000, 49

Webb, S (1901). *The Case for the Factory Acts*. Grant Richards, London.

Wright, Maureen. (2011). *Elizabeth Wolstenholme Elmy and the Victorian Feminist Movement: the Biography of an Insurgent Woman*. Manchester University Press.

Other resources

https://www.bl.uk/collection-items/the-subjection-of-women-by-j-s-mill

https://www.bl.uk/votes-for-women/articles/womens-suffrage-key-figures

https://www.civilservant.org.uk/women-history.html

https://www.victorianvoices.net/topics/work/clerical.html

Women's Emancipation Union, report of inaugural meeting, October 1892. Accessed: 21/08/2021 at https://archive.org/details/womensemancipati00wome/page/n7/mode/2up

Women's Franchise League. Report of proceedings at Inaugural meeting. London, 25 July, 1889. Accessed: 21/08/2021 at https://digital.library.lse.ac.uk/objects/lse:tab479dof/read/single#page/1/mode/1up

Celebrating Elizabeth

Women today still need opportunities and support to build on the work of Elizabeth and other Victorian feminists. All profits from the sale of this book will go to two charities that represent her work.

Futures for Women: SPEW was set up in 1859 to provide women with opportunities to gain training and to enter employment. The work of this organisation continues today, now under the name of Futures for Women.
https://futuresforwomen.org.uk/history/

Moravian Women's Association (MWA): Following her two years' education at Fulneck Moravian School, Elizabeth made significant contributions to education both locally and nationally. Today the MWA supports women locally and internationally to improve their lives and to enable them to become independent.

Further research

While working on this book I have become fascinated by the work of Josephine Butler and her friendship with Elizabeth. This will be the next focus of my work. To join in the story please subscribe for my newsletter at www.elizabethwe. co.uk/postings/ or email me at mary@woodhall28.co.uk.

You may also wish to email me to book a talk about Elizabeth and her many campaigns.

Author's biography

Dr Mary Holmes has lived much of her life in Leeds, while travelling extensively throughout the UK with her business. As a young person she spent a brief period teaching abroad with Voluntary Services Overseas; this strengthened her commitment to women's rights which drove her commitment to equality in the workplace.

Living in Yorkshire allows Mary to indulge her love of walking in the countryside. She also enjoys reading and is actively involved in the theatre. It was during her work on a Fulneck Heritage Open Day exhibition that she first discovered Elizabeth Wolstenholme Elmy.